newSOUL cooking

newSOUL cooking

updating a cuisine rich in flavor and tradition

TANYA HOLLAND

photographs by **Ellen Silverman**

stewart, tabori & chang   new york

Text copyright © 2003 Tanya Holland
Photographs copyright © 2003 Ellen Silverman
Food stylist: Susie Theodorou

Photography prop credits: orange bowl (on page 87), cream plate (on page 109), and beakers (on page 132) from MUD Australia. Available through The Brandman Agency, 245 Fifth Avenue, Suite 602, New York, NY 10016, tel. (212) 683-2442; www.brandmanpr.com.

Project editor: Sandra Gilbert
Production: Kim Tyner and Alexis Mentor

Published by
Stewart, Tabori & Chang
A Company of La Martinière Groupe
115 West 18th Street
New York, NY 10011

Export Sales to all countries except Canada,
France, and French-speaking Switzerland:
Thames and Hudson Ltd.
181A High Holborn
London WC1V 7QX
England

Canadian Distribution:
Canadian Manda Group
One Atlantic Avenue, Suite 105
Toronto, Ontario M6K 3E7
Canada

Library of Congress Cataloging-in-Publication Data
Holland, Tanya
          New soul cooking : updating a cuisine rich in flavor and tradition / Tanya Holland ; photographs by Ellen Silverman.
                    p. cm.
Includes index.
ISBN 1-58479-289-2
1.   African American cookery. I. Title.

TX715.H733 2003
641.59'296073—dc21   2003044901

The text of this book was composed in Folio and Caecilia.

DESIGN BY NINA BARNETT

Printed in Singapore
10 9 8 7 6 5 4 3 2

This book is dedicated to the memory
of my grandmothers—
for their love, encouragement,
and inspiration.

Martha Norwood Thomas

March 9, 1917–September 29, 2002

and

Flora Tyree Holland

October 12, 1920–January 20, 2003

contents

INTRODUCTION

Soul food is a term that was coined in the 1960s and refers to the foods common in African-American communities that connect people to their shared roots. This cuisine combines the staples that were used by many generations of cooks in the South of the United States, whose ancestors brought exotic ingredients from Africa to the New World, and the ingredients indigenous to America. The term emerged at the same time as soul music, which was based on gospel and rhythm & blues. Indeed, cooking and creating music are closely related, since they both can involve improvising with ingredients or material on hand.

New Soul cooking is my interpretation of soul food. When I was growing up, some of the food my family ate was different from that of friends and neighbors of European, Latin, and Asian descent. When my parents prepared collard greens, corn bread, or grits, for example, I could always tell that they felt a little more at home: Rochester, New York, where I was raised, was far away, both in distance and culturally, from the rural areas of Virginia and Louisiana where they were brought up.

The flavors of the American South, Africa, and Brazil are the basis for New Soul cooking. This book also incorporates influences from the Caribbean Islands of Jamaica, Guadeloupe, Trinidad, Haiti, and other smaller islands where many people are descendants of the Africans transported during the transatlantic slave trade from the 1520s to the 1860s. New Soul cooking uses the traditional ingredients associated with soul food, such as black-eyed peas, okra, and sweet potatoes, with the addition of other ingredients, such as pomegranate molasses and rice-wine vinegar, to create a global cuisine.

I prefer to cook with seasonal and fresh ingredients, while applying both classic and modern cooking techniques. My culinary training in France, where many cooks and restaurants prepare foods from their own gardens, as well as a personal reflection on the more health-conscious way we eat today influenced much of my interpretation. Here you will find recipes with bold flavors, but little or none of the animal-fat content found in traditional soul food.

This cookbook is divided into chapters that reflect dining courses, reminiscent of the European-style meals I've enjoyed. I've also discovered that people around the United States use different names to refer to certain parts of a meal. However, traditional soul food was hardly ever served in courses. People usually gathered at a large buffet table (if the pots even actually left the stove) and filled their dishes.

I prefer to eat in courses because it creates an element of surprise, more variety in flavors, and portions tend to be smaller. I serve an appetizer or salad first, followed by a simply prepared meat or fish entrée with a starch and vegetables, all on one plate. And as is traditional, the dessert course always stands on its own. This format allows cooks and chefs to have fun with presentation. And as a diner, I'm always amazed at the many ways dishes are interpreted.

New Soul Cooking is for seasoned cooks who want to modernize their favorite dishes and also for the younger generation that may not have had the opportunity to learn from their parents and grandparents. This book is also for every cooking enthusiast who looks for new culinary perspectives and are especially interested in the ethnic cuisine of their own heritage and that of other cultures.

THE NEW SOUL PANTRY

Stocking your pantry is the first place to increase your culinary vocabulary. Many of the ingredients that I keep on hand are listed below. Some of these ingredients are familiar and expected; others will add a brand-new dimension to your cooking and eating experience. The soul-food pantry, traditional and New, is what makes this cuisine come alive and forms the basis of my recipes. This list is not comprehensive, but it's a great place to start.

Benne seeds Benne and sesame seeds are one and the same. *Benne* is the name that the West Africans called these seeds that they brought to the American South.

Black-eyed peas This off-white legume with a black "eye" in the center has a subtle green-pea taste. It is a good source of protein.

Brown sugar The rich, molasses flavor adds depth to recipes where granulated sugar is suggested. I specify light or dark in each recipe when the difference is important.

Chiles There are so many different types of fresh and dried chiles. More are available regularly in local grocery stores. Since you may need some help differentiating between the types, here's a short list of some of my favorites, which are used in several of the recipes.

Ancho A dried, smoked poblano chile
Chipotle A dried, smoked jalapeño chile, often found in adobo sauce
Habanero A small, round chile, one of the hottest
Jalapeño The one chile most people know best; its heat varies
Poblano A flavorful, long, dark-green chile with heat that varies
Scotch bonnet A Jamaican favorite; besides the habanero, the other hot, hot one
Serrano A small, hot green chile
Thai One of the smallest (about 1 to 1½ inches), and very hot. They can be used when green or when further ripened and red, and are easily found in most supermarkets or Asian grocers.

When working with chile peppers, wear latex gloves, or use a fork and knife to cut them. If you do happen to touch them with bare hands, keep your hands away from your face and wash them immediately after you've finished prepping the chiles.

Chocolate Some of the highest-quality cocoa beans are grown in Ghana, a small country in northwest Africa. I like to use a high-quality bittersweet chocolate and cocoa powder combination, such as Scharffen Berger or Valrhona.

Filé powder A specialty dried spice made of sassafras leaves ground into a powder. It is used as a flavoring and a thickening agent in Creole and Cajun cuisine.

Green onions A green onion has a bulbous root like a scallion. Many people confuse scallions with green onions, but a true scallion has a base with straight sides and green onions ordinarily are slightly curved, showing the beginning of a bulb. Some people mix up the scallion with the shallot, a small, sweet bulb that looks rather like a small onion. In New Soul Cooking green onions are interchangeable with scallions. Use both white and green parts unless otherwise specified.

Grits Corn was a special gift from the Native Americans to the Colonists. Grits are ground hominy, the name for ground, dried white or yellow corn kernels that have had the husk and germ removed either mechanically or by soaking them in lye. This coarse earthy grain has been a staple in the South for generations.

Herbs There is no substitute for fresh herbs, which are best added toward the end of the cooking process. Some of my favorites are thyme, parsley, basil, chervil, cilantro, and sage.

Molasses The first product in the sugar-making process, molasses is created when the juice is squeezed from sugarcane and boiled to make a dark-brown syrup. The crystals are removed and become either brown or granulated sugar. Because of the intensity of its flavor, a little goes a long way.

Oils Buy the best-quality oils for cooking that you can find, especially when using them for vinaigrettes. Some examples are extra-virgin olive oil, canola oil, sesame oil, and grapeseed oil.

Okra A fruit with many edible seeds inside its pod, okra is at its peak flavor during the summer. It is delicious quickly sautéed and served with fresh tomatoes.

Pecans These nuts are pervasive in Southern cuisine primarily because the trees on which they grow thrive in warmer climates. They've been incorporated into sweet specialties such as pralines and pecan pie, but they also enhance many savory recipes.

Pomegranate molasses You can find this wonderful ingredient in Middle Eastern markets and gourmet stores. It's a reduction of fresh pomegranate juice that is rich and sweet.

Rice My friend Braima Moiwa, a food and cultural historian from Sierra Leone, tells me that the first rice cultivated in the Carolinas resembled basmati rice, which is similar to the rice that the Africans brought to this country. The different varieties available today developed over time. I always keep a selection of long-grain, basmati, jasmine, brown, and wild rice in my pantry.

Spices The shelf life of dried spices is limited, so buy them in small amounts. Dried spices are great for rubs and marinades. Some important ones to have on hand are thyme, oregano, garlic powder, onion powder, mustard, nutmeg, allspice, cinnamon, and ginger.

Sweet potatoes and yams These two varieties of potatoes have confused many people. The sweet potato belongs to the morning glory family (*Convolvulaceae*) and is native to the Americas. The yam is derived from an ancient species (*Dioscorea batatas*) that has been cultivated in Africa and Asia for many centuries. They are interchangeable in most recipes, but I recommend the less starchy sweet potato when making desserts.

Vanilla Good-quality pure vanilla extract or beans from Madagascar, off the southeast coast of Africa, are the best. The beans will give a stronger flavor and it is up to the cook whether they wish to see the tiny specks in their dish.

Vidalia onions These sweet onions are native to Georgia. They are great in salads where raw white or red onions can be too strong. Different sweet onion varieties can be found in other parts of the country—such as Walla Walla onions from Washington and Maui onions from the Hawaiian Islands. Feel free to substitute Vidalia onions with other varieties in *New Soul Cooking* recipes.

Vinegars I like to keep a variety of flavored vinegars on hand, such as apple cider, rice wine, balsamic, champagne, and red wine.

appetizers,
FIRST COURSES,
starters,
SMALL PLATES,
soups, SALADS

I once had an employer who compared the work in a restaurant to that of the theater—the first seating of customers is, naturally, show time! The appetizer, first course, or starter sets the stage for the rest of the meal, the whole of which is a subtle drama achieved through presentation and service. In the best situation, diners leave the table feeling entertained, but not overwhelmed. Keep this in mind the next time you host a dinner party or even a more intimate affair—the small dishes here give a tantalizing hint of the food to come by their unique blend of traditional bistro fare happily married to familiar soul-food cooking.

gingered yellow sweet potato soup

Makes eight 1¼-cup servings

Ginger reminds me of the islands—the Caribbean islands from Jamaica to Trinidad and all the beautiful ones in between—and its taste is ubiquitous throughout the cuisine, from beverages to desserts. I love starting with a bite of ginger to stimulate the palate, and here it provides a delightful contrast when mixed into the silky sweet potato puree. The yellow sweet potato variety has less natural sugar than the orange-fleshed kind so you won't feel as if you're starting with dessert.

3½ pounds (about 4 large) yellow
   sweet potatoes, peeled and cut into
   1-inch cubes
1 teaspoon coarse salt, plus more to taste
2 tablespoons unsalted butter
2 onions, minced (about 2 cups)
1 clove garlic, minced
1 piece (1½ inches) fresh ginger, minced
¼ teaspoon ground ginger
1 cinnamon stick
Freshly ground white pepper, to taste
Honey, to taste
½ cup heavy cream
Chervil, chives, or parsley, for garnish

Place sweet potatoes in a large pot and cover with water; add 1 teaspoon salt. Bring to a boil; reduce heat to medium, and cook, uncovered, until fork-tender, about 15 minutes. Meanwhile, in a medium skillet over low heat, melt butter; add onions, garlic, and fresh ginger. Cook until soft and translucent, about 15 minutes.

Drain potatoes, reserving the cooking liquid. Transfer 1 cup sweet potatoes and 1 cup cooking liquid to blender. Add ¼ cup onion mixture, and blend, covered, until smooth. Pour the potato mixture into a large bowl. Repeat until all the potatoes are blended.

Using a fine sieve, strain the puree into a clean, large pot. Heat the puree over low heat, and season with ground ginger, cinnamon stick, salt, white pepper, and honey. Cook 30 minutes, until the flavors blend, and then stir in heavy cream. Remove cinnamon stick. Garnish with herbs and serve immediately.

black-eyed pea and country ham chowder

Makes eight 1¼-cup servings

The different textures—from the chunks of potatoes to the savory bits of ham—in this chowder make this a great one-pot meal or a hearty starter. This dish is a great new way to eat black-eyed peas for good luck in the New Year, a tradition throughout the American South. This recipe tastes great without adding salt because of the saltiness of the ham.

2 tablespoons unsalted butter

1½ cup minced onions

1 clove garlic, minced

1½ tablespoons jalapeño chile
   (about 1 large), seeded and minced

1 cup diced celery

1 cup diced carrots

1 cup diced cooked country ham
   (about 1½ pounds)

2 cups chicken stock

1 tablespoon chopped thyme

¾ teaspoon celery seeds

½ teaspoon freshly ground white pepper

1 bay leaf

1½ pounds dried black-eyed peas,
   soaked overnight

2 cups Yukon Gold potatoes, peeled and
   diced small

1 cup half-and-half

In a large pot, melt butter over medium heat. Add onions, garlic, and jalapeño. Cook for 5 minutes until soft; add celery, carrots, and ham. Stir in chicken stock, thyme, celery seeds, white pepper, bay leaf, and black-eyed peas, and bring to a boil. Reduce to simmer, and cook 20 minutes; add potatoes. Simmer an additional 25 minutes, and add half-and-half. Adjust seasoning as desired. Serve immediately.

baby spinach salad

with lardons, vidalia onions, apple dressing, and blue cheese croutons

Makes 6 servings

I created this salad to combine two of my favorite influences, ingredients from the New Soul pantry and a touch of French bistro cuisine. One of the most enticing pleasures of New Soul cooking is the way each ingredient has a unique integrity that is maintained when combined: the greens are fresh and delicate; the Vidalia onion is tender yet crunchy; and the salty, creamy blue cheese beautifully offsets the apple's sweetness. And the thick-cut bacon, or *lardons* in French, adds a meaty bite.

½ pound slab or thick-cut bacon (lardons),
    cut into ¼-inch dice
1 cup apples, peeled and chopped into
    ½-inch pieces
1 tablespoon chopped shallots
1 teaspoon minced garlic
1 tablespoon fresh thyme leaves
1 cup apple cider or unfiltered apple juice
¼ cup apple cider vinegar
½ cup canola oil
¼ cup extra-virgin olive oil, plus more
    for drizzling
Coarse salt
Freshly ground white pepper
6 slices white bread
Freshly ground black pepper, to taste
6 to 8 ounces Fourme d'Ambert or other
    blue cheese

2 pounds baby spinach, washed and dried
1 Vidalia onion, thinly sliced

LARDONS Bring a small pot of water to a boil. Add bacon and let water return to a boil. Boil 2 minutes, strain, and repeat process. Dry bacon on a paper towel. Heat a heavy skillet over medium high heat; add bacon and cook until crisp. Remove excess fat and drain bacon on a paper towel; set aside.

APPLE DRESSING In a small saucepan over medium heat, cook apples, shallots, garlic, thyme leaves, and apple cider about 15 minutes, or until apples are tender and most of the liquid has evaporated. In a blender or small food processor, add apple mixture and apple cider vinegar, and with blender running, slowly add oils in a steady stream until dressing is smooth. Season to taste with salt and white pepper; set aside.

BLUE CHEESE CROUTONS Preheat the oven to 250°F. Cut crusts off of the bread slices. Cut each slice into 4 triangles. Place bread on a baking sheet, and drizzle olive oil and season with salt and black pepper. Toast bread slices 3 minutes; rotate slices and toast an additional 3 minutes. Set aside.

Preheat the broiler. Slice the cheese into triangles to cover toast (or crumble to generously cover), and place on toast. Broil 1 minute, or until cheese melts; be careful not to let the croutons burn.

To serve Toss bacon, spinach, and onion slices with the dressing. Divide among six plates and arrange the croutons evenly around each.

pickled vegetable salad
with crumbled goat cheese and peppercress

Makes 6 servings

I can hardly imagine a Southern meal without a pickled vegetable or condiment on the table. You can buy pickling spice premade or easily assemble it as needed. The main ingredients are peppercorns, bay leaf, and cloves, but some people add mustard seeds or coriander seeds. When choosing spices, consider which ones best complement the vegetables you're pickling. Savory, mellow goat cheese is a perfect foil for the sweet, tangy flavor of the pickled vegetables.

1 tablespoon coarse salt, plus more to taste
1 cup cauliflower florets
1 cup (about ⅓ pound) haricots verts
   (French green beans), ends trimmed
1 cup pearl onions, peeled
2 beets, peeled and quartered
Pickling Liquid (recipe follows)
2 tablespoons extra-virgin olive oil
Freshly ground black pepper
1 pound peppercress, or other baby- or
   micro greens (such as beet or pea greens)
4 ounces soft goat cheese, crumbled

Bring a large pot of water to a boil, and add 1 tablespoon salt. Prepare a large bowl of ice water, and set aside. Cook the cauliflower 3 minutes, or until fork-tender. With a slotted spoon, transfer florets to ice water; allow to cool completely. Drain in colander. Repeat the process with the haricots verts (they should be bright green and tender) and pearl onions. Place beets in a small pot and cover with water; bring to a boil, and cook about 15 minutes, or until fork-tender. Drain beets.

Layer the vegetables into a 2-quart pickling jar. Reserve ¼ cup pickling liquid, and pour the remainder over the vegetables. Let the vegetables stand, refrigerated, overnight, or at least 4 hours.

Whisk olive oil into the reserved pickling liquid to make vinaigrette. Toss with greens, and season with salt and black pepper to taste. Arrange vegetables on plate with greens in the center and sprinkle goat cheese on top. Extra vegetables will keep up to one week in the refrigerator.

PICKLING LIQUID
Makes about 3 cups

1½ cups cider vinegar
1½ cups water
¾ cup sugar
2 bay leaves
2 tablespoons coarse salt
2 cloves garlic
1 tablespoon whole coriander
2 teaspoons white peppercorns
1 teaspoon whole cloves

In a large pot, bring all ingredients to a boil. Stir to combine. While liquid is hot, pour over vegetables.

wilted watercress salad

with sesame-ginger vinaigrette and oranges

Makes 4 servings

This salad is slightly Asian influenced with the tastes of shiitake mushrooms and rice-wine vinegar, but it highlights the African contribution of benne, or sesame seeds. Watercress is a hearty, peppery-tasting green in the mustard family. The texture and flavor of its distinctive leaves are perfect in a wilted salad with other zesty ingredients.

1 tablespoon sesame oil
1 tablespoon canola oil
1 teaspoon minced garlic
1 piece (1 inch) fresh ginger, grated
½ pound shiitake mushrooms
½ red onion, thinly sliced
⅓ cup rice-wine vinegar
3 oranges, cut into segments, juice reserved
2 bunches watercress, cleaned with large stems removed
2 tablespoons toasted sesame seeds
Coarse salt
Freshly ground black pepper

Heat sesame and canola oils in a medium skillet over medium-high heat. Add garlic, ginger, and mushrooms. Cook 2 minutes, or until vegetables are soft. (The mushrooms will absorb most of the oil.) Add onion, vinegar, and orange juice. Cook vegetables 3 to 4 minutes, or until onion is soft. Place watercress in a bowl and toss with the mushroom mixture. Add orange segments and sesame seeds; season with salt and pepper to taste.

virginia ham, vidalia onion, and asiago tart

Makes 8 servings

This is a simple dish that's great as a starter or a complete meal with the addition of a small salad or greens. Virginia ham is also known as Smithfield ham after the town in Virginia where the grain-fed hogs are raised, butchered, smoked, and cured. This process also involves the addition of special seasoning to give the ham its unique flavor. The surprisingly sweet Vidalia onion partners well with the saltiness in the ham. Aged Asiago cheese, one of my favorites, is a reasonably priced hard cheese that adds a delicious sharp bite.

2 tablespoons vegetable oil
1 Vidalia onion, thinly sliced
Pastry Dough (recipe follows)
1½ cups heavy cream
3 large eggs
3 large egg yolks
½ teaspoon coarse salt
¼ teaspoon freshly ground white pepper
Pinch freshly grated nutmeg
½ pound cooked country ham, thinly sliced
½ cup grated aged Asiago cheese
2 tablespoons chopped fresh parsley

Preheat the oven to 350°F. In a large skillet over medium heat, heat oil. Cook onion 10 minutes, or until soft; set aside to cool.

On a work surface dusted with flour, roll out the dough to fit a 10-inch tart pan. Transfer to pan, and trim edges with a sharp knife if necessary. Line with foil. On top of the foil, fill the crust with pie weights or dried beans, and bake 10 minutes, or until lightly browned. Remove from oven, and remove weights and foil; set aside. In a mixing bowl, whisk cream, eggs, yolks, salt, white pepper, and nutmeg; set aside. Reduce oven to 325°F. Arrange onion and ham evenly in crust, and pour cream mixture over top. Mix cheese and parsley, and sprinkle mixture on top of filling. Bake 25 to 30 minutes, until egg filling is set and top is lightly browned.

PASTRY DOUGH

Makes one 10-inch tart

2¼ cups all-purpose flour
1½ sticks unsalted butter,
  diced and chilled
1 teaspoon coarse salt

Place the flour, butter, and salt into the bowl of a
food processor. Pulse until butter is approximately
the size of small peas. Slowly add 5 to 7 tablespoons of iced water until the dough forms into a
ball. Wrap the dough ball tightly in plastic, and
chill at least 30 minutes, up to 1 hour.

spiced molasses duck breast salad with figs, pecans, and bitter greens

Makes 4 servings

When I smell ginger, cinnamon, and molasses, I'm instantly transported to the Caribbean islands, where sugarcane products and aromatic spices infuse the cuisine. And figs remind me of the tree in my grandmother's backyard in Louisiana—which she used to make something memorable, such as chunky fig preserves. This delicate, sensual combination is New Soul cooking at its best.

1 piece (3 inches) fresh ginger, minced

2 tablespoons minced garlic

Zest of 1 orange

⅓ cup molasses

⅓ cup pomegranate molasses

⅓ cup pure maple syrup

½ cup soy sauce

1 cup canola oil

2 pieces star anise

2 cinnamon sticks

1 teaspoon freshly ground black pepper, plus more to taste

4 boneless Long Island duck breasts, skin scored and excess fat removed

1 head frisee

2 heads endive

½ pound Upland or other baby cress

1 cup dried Calmyrna figs, stemmed and quartered

½ cup pecan pieces, toasted

Coarse salt, to taste

SPICED MOLASSES DUCK Whisk ginger, garlic, zest, molasses, pomegranate molasses, maple syrup, soy sauce, oil, star anise, cinnamon sticks, and 1 teaspoon pepper together in a bowl. Strain ½ cup of the mixture, and set aside. Place the duck in a shallow dish; add remaining marinade, and cover with plastic wrap. Refrigerate for 6 hours or up to overnight.

Preheat the oven to 350°F. Remove duck from the marinade. Heat a large ovenproof skillet over medium-high heat, and cook duck skin side down until most of the fat is rendered, about 3 minutes. Turn and sear the other side 1 minute; pour off excess fat. Transfer the duck to the oven and cook until medium rare, approximately 1½ minutes (when touched, meat will lightly bounce back). Allow duck to rest 1 minute before slicing.

To serve Clean and tear frisee into bite-size pieces, separate endive, and clean cress. Toss greens with reserved dressing, figs, and pecans. Season to taste with salt and pepper. Slice each breast crosswise into 6 pieces. Place greens in a mound in the center of 4 plates, and arrange duck around the outsides.

jerked prawns

Makes 4 servings

Jerk spice has a unique taste—a mixture of hot chile peppers and warm spices such as nutmeg, cinnamon, and allspice that Americans usually associate with desserts. Jerk spice was originally used by Jamaicans as a method for preserving meats, but today, *jerk* refers to a particular seasoning and cooking method of meats, seafood, poultry, or vegetables when using a chile-based marinade or rub. The Scotch bonnet is the favorite chile in Jamaica, but any fresh hot chile will do.

4 teaspoons ground allspice
2 teaspoons cayenne pepper
2 teaspoons ground nutmeg
2 teaspoons ground cinnamon
1 tablespoon garlic powder
1 tablespoon onion powder
2 teaspoons coarse salt
1 teaspoon ground cascabel chile
  (or other hot chile)
1 teaspoon freshly ground black pepper
1 cup cider vinegar
½ cup soy sauce
½ cup vegetable oil
¼ cup water
1 red onion, sliced into thin rings
1 head garlic, peeled and sliced thin

1 Scotch bonnet or habanero chile,
  seeded and sliced into thin rings
2 jalapeño chiles, seeded and sliced into
  thin rings
2 pounds prawns, peeled and deveined

Mix together the allspice, cayenne, nutmeg, cinnamon, garlic and onion powders, salt, chile, and black pepper in a large bowl; then slowly whisk in cider vinegar, soy sauce, vegetable oil, and the water. Add onion, garlic, and chiles. Add the prawns to the jerk mixture to marinate and refrigerate 2 to 6 hours. Grill or broil prawns until just cooked through, 4 to 5 minutes. Serve immediately.

poached salmon–and–potato cakes

Makes 12 cakes

This dish reminds me of Saturday brunches growing up, when my dad usually served canned salmon with scrambled eggs. Even though the range of my tastes has expanded, I often return to these well-loved flavors and textures. This is a great way to use leftover mashed potatoes, too. I like to make these cakes when crab is not in season, and it's a less expensive substitute. The Roasted Tomato Mayonnaise on page 141 is a wonderful condiment for this dish.

2 pounds skinless salmon fillet

1 teaspoon cayenne pepper

Coarse salt, to taste

Freshly ground white pepper, to taste

½ cup dry white wine

⅔ cup minced onion

2 teaspoons minced garlic

1½ cups chilled mashed potatoes

¼ cup chopped fresh herbs (such as parsley, basil, chives, or tarragon)

¾ to 1 cup dried bread crumbs

3 tablespoons vegetable oil

3 tablespoons unsalted butter

Preheat the oven to 350°F. Season the salmon with cayenne and salt and white pepper to taste. In a baking dish, place fish with wine, onion, and garlic; bake 7 minutes, or until cooked through. When fish is completely cool, mix with potatoes and the herbs. Drain off any access liquid. In your palm, form ¼ cup of the mixture into a 2-inch patty, and roll in bread crumbs. Repeat to make 12 cakes total.

In a large skillet over medium-high heat, add 1 tablespoon oil and 1 tablespoon butter. When the oil is hot, cook as many salmon cakes as will fit in the pan without crowding, about 2 minutes on each side. Transfer to a baking sheet lined with paper towels. Repeat for all cakes. After all salmon cakes are toasted, remove the paper towels, and place the cakes in the oven 10 minutes to heat through. Serve immediately.

sweet potato blinis
with bourbon-cured salmon and caviar

Makes 36 blinis

Every soul food menu has a sweet potato recipe, usually in the form of a baked, sweetened side dish. This nontraditional dish was inspired by my experience with Russian culture and cuisine. I've exchanged sweet potato puree for the buckwheat flour usually used to make these small savory pancakes. I like to serve them with salmon that is cured with bourbon, a corn whiskey produced in the South, where soul food originated. This dish makes a hearty first course or great cocktail-size minis. I prefer to use American hackleback or salmon roe to avoid overharvested varieties of caviar.

2 large sweet potatoes, peeled and cut into
  2-inch pieces
1½ teaspoons coarse salt
2 tablespoons honey
8 tablespoons (1 stick) unsalted butter,
  softened
1 cup milk
2 large eggs, lightly beaten
1½ cups all-purpose flour
1 tablespoon baking powder
½ teaspoon cayenne pepper
½ pound bourbon-cured salmon, thinly sliced
  (recipe follows)
¼ cup crème fraîche
2 ounces caviar
Dill sprigs, for garnish

Place the sweet potatoes in a medium saucepan and add enough water to cover by 1 inch. Add ½ teaspoon salt. Bring to a boil over medium heat, and cook until the potatoes are very tender when pierced with a fork, about 10 minutes. Drain well and return potatoes to the saucepan. Add honey and 4 tablespoons butter. Transfer mixture to a food processor, and puree. In a small bowl, combine the milk and eggs, and stir into the sweet potato puree. In another bowl, stir together the flour, baking powder, the remaining 1 teaspoon salt, and cayenne. Add the dry ingredients to the sweet potatoes, and stir just until blended.

Melt the remaining 4 tablespoons butter, and set aside. Heat 2 large nonstick skillets over medium heat and coat them lightly with melted butter. Drop heaping tablespoons of sweet-potato mixture into the skillets to form a 2-inch blini; repeat with as many as will fit in the skillets. Turn once and press down slightly, cooking until golden and crisp, about 2 minutes per side. Transfer blinis to a large foil-lined baking sheet. Repeat to form 36 blinis. The blinis can sit at room temperature up to 2 hours; heat through in a 350°F oven 5 minutes before serving.

To serve Arrange 3 blinis on a plate and garnish each with a slice of cured salmon, a dollop of crème fraîche, a small spoonful (less than ½ teaspoon) of caviar, and dill sprigs.

BOURBON-CURED SALMON
Makes 12 servings

1½ cups packed brown sugar
1 cup coarse salt
½ cup good-quality bourbon
2 tablespoons mustard seeds
2 tablespoons hot-pepper sauce
   (such as Tabasco)
1 tablespoon Dijon-style mustard
¼ cup chopped dill
1 to 1½ pounds salmon side or fillet,
   skin left on

Combine all ingredients except salmon in a bowl; stir until mixture forms thin paste. Place the salmon in a shallow dish, and pour curing mixture over salmon. Cover with plastic wrap, pressing the plastic against the fish. Weigh down fish with a heavy pan (a cast-iron skillet works well). Refrigerate for 48 hours. Scrape off the curing mixture with a paper towel. Cut the salmon against the grain, slicing into thin pieces.

piri piri grilled shrimp
with mango dipping sauce

Makes 6 to 8 servings

Piri piri is the name of a dish indigenous to Mozambique, a southeastern African nation, which is one of the largest exporters of shrimp in the world. Piri piri is also the name of a small, potent red chile, similar to small red chiles we find in supermarkets. Because they are hard to find in the United States, Thai chiles make a good substitute. This dish makes a great cocktail food when served on skewers and covered with the cooling Mango Dipping Sauce.

16 (10-inch) wooden skewers
1 pound large shrimp, cleaned and
  deveined with tails attached
1 can (8 ounces) unsweetened coconut milk
1 tablespoon minced garlic
3 Thai chiles (or piri piri chiles), finely chopped
Zest of 1 lime
½ teaspoon paprika
Coarse salt
Freshly ground white pepper
2 tablespoons vegetable oil
Mango Dipping Sauce (recipe follows)

To prevent skewers from burning on the grill, soak them in water 30 minutes, and then drain. Place 3 shrimp on each skewer and put in a shallow dish with sides. Whisk together coconut milk, garlic, chiles, zest, and paprika, and pour over shrimp. Marinate overnight or at least 6 hours.

Preheat the grill or grill pan over high heat. Drain shrimp and season generously with salt and pepper; toss in vegetable oil and skewer. Grill 1½ minutes on both sides, or until shrimp are opaque and cooked through. Serve with Mango Dipping Sauce.

MANGO DIPPING SAUCE
Makes about 1½ cups

½ mango, peeled
1 tablespoon freshly squeezed lime juice
1 cup red-wine vinegar
½ cup sugar
½ red bell pepper, cored, seeded, and diced
½ green bell pepper, cored, seeded, and diced

Place the mango and lime juice in a blender or food processor, and puree. Bring vinegar and sugar to a boil, and then reduce heat to medium; cook until it becomes thick and syrupy. Remove the mixture from heat and let cool; when completely cool, add to blender with mango puree. Pour into bowl and mix in diced bell peppers.

island-spiced braised beef short ribs

Makes 8 servings

I like using this fragrant glaze instead of traditional barbecue sauce to keep things interesting. A short rib appetizer is a hearty starter, but the Tropical Salsa found on page 144 balances the richness of the ribs. Use the most exotic fruits you can find, such as papaya, mango, and carambola—the tastes will evoke an island beach cookout on a calm, clear night.

1½ tablespoons ground allspice
1½ tablespoons ground cinnamon
1½ tablespoons ground star anise
1½ tablespoons freshly ground black pepper
1½ tablespoons ground fennel seeds
¼ cup minced garlic
¾ cup canola oil
½ cup soy sauce
3 tablespoons honey
1 Scotch bonnet chile, seeded and quartered
Coarse salt, to taste
5 pounds beef short ribs, cut into 2-inch
   pieces
1½ quarts of beef stock or broth

Mix allspice, cinnamon, star anise, pepper, fennel seeds, garlic, canola oil, soy sauce, honey, chile, and salt in a bowl large enough to fit the ribs. Add ribs and allow them to marinate overnight or at least 6 hours in refrigerator.

Preheat the oven to 325°F. Remove ribs from marinade, reserving the chile pieces, and season generously with salt. Place ribs in a roasting pan large enough to hold the ribs plus the stock without spilling. Add the stock, ribs, and reserved chile pieces. Cook ribs for 2½ hours, or until ribs are tender and the meat pulls easily from the bone. Serve 1 rib per person.

cornmeal-coated fried oysters

Makes 24 oysters

This dish reminds me of my first trip to New Orleans, where I discovered that the French influence in the cuisine is very obvious, especially with the sauces served with dishes. Rémoulade is a classic French sauce served with chilled seafood, and I like to use it with this dish. Here, the cooking process is so quick that the oysters are still chilled in the center and the cornmeal absorbs very little oil. Having the correct oil temperature is the most important step in this recipe to keep the oysters ethereally crispy and light.

1½ cups all-purpose flour
Coarse salt, to taste
Freshly ground white pepper, to taste
2 large eggs
2 tablespoons milk
1½ cups cornmeal
Cayenne pepper, to taste
2 dozen freshly shucked oysters (clean
    and reserve shell bottoms for serving)
½ cup vegetable oil
Spicy Rémoulade (see recipe, page 140)
Italian parsley leaves, for garnish

In a small bowl, combine flour, salt, and white pepper. In another small bowl, whisk together eggs and milk. In a third small bowl, combine cornmeal, salt, white pepper, and cayenne. Dip oysters in flour mixture, then egg mixture, and then cornmeal mixture.

Heat skillet over medium heat, and add ¼ cup vegetable oil. The oil should be at 375°F on a deep fat thermometer. Make sure the oil is not smoking. Add 6 oysters (do not overcrowd skillet), and cook for about 2 minutes on each side. Drain on clean paper towels. Repeat for remaining oysters, using the remaining ½ cup oil as needed.

To serve Spoon a heaping teaspoon Spicy Rémoulade on the bottom of each cleaned oyster shell. Top with an oyster, and garnish with parsley.

pepperpot shrimp cakes

Makes 6 servings

Pepperpot is a one-dish Jamaican specialty made with meat, greens, potatoes, and hot chiles, and here I incorporate these flavors into a compact bite of these shrimp cakes. The sweet and spicy combination balanced with cooling coconut milk creates a pleasing sensation. Serve these with New Soul Hot Red Pepper Sauce found on page 138.

1 can (12 ounces) coconut milk

1 cinnamon stick

3 whole cloves

1 tablespoon minced red jalapeño chile

1 piece (1 inch) fresh ginger, peeled
   and chopped

4 cloves garlic, chopped

Zest of 2 limes, about 1 teaspoon

2½ pounds shrimp, peeled and deveined

2 sweet potatoes, peeled and diced small

2 Idaho or russet potatoes, peeled and
   diced small

½ cup water

3 pounds mustard greens

1½ pounds spinach

2 bunches green onions, chopped

3 large eggs

⅓ cup mayonnaise

1⅓ cups dried fine bread crumbs

2 tablespoons chopped fresh thyme

Coarse salt

Freshly ground white pepper

1 cup canola oil

In a medium saucepan, add coconut milk, cinnamon stick, cloves, jalapeño, ginger, garlic, and zest, and bring to a boil. Add shrimp and lower heat to a simmer; cook until shrimp is pink and opaque, for about 2 minutes. Remove from heat, and let shrimp cool in liquid so flavors blend. Cook sweet and Idaho potatoes in separate pots with salted water until fork-tender; set aside. In a large pot, heat the water over medium heat; add mustard greens, spinach, and green onions, and cook until completely wilted. Let cool. Drain, squeeze out water, and finely chop.

In a small bowl, combine eggs, mayonnaise, and ⅓ cup bread crumbs; set aside. Strain the cooled shrimp and discard liquid; chop the shrimp into small pieces. In a large bowl, combine shrimp, potatoes, chopped greens mixture, thyme, and egg mixture. Season to taste with salt and pepper. Shape the mixture into 2-inch cakes and then roll in the remaining bread crumbs.

Preheat the oven to 350°F. Add 3 tablespoons of oil to a large skillet over medium-high heat. Cook 6 shrimp cakes at a time (do not overcrowd skillet) 2 minutes on each side and then transfer to baking sheet. Repeat for all shrimp. Transfer the browned shrimp to oven for 5 minutes to warm through.

brown sugar and pineapple-glazed spare ribs

Makes 8 servings

These might possibly be the juiciest ribs you'll ever taste. The slow-cooking method of using low heat over a long period makes the meat on these ribs fall right off the bone. The sweet-heat flavor is my favorite part of this Caribbean-inspired dish. Pineapples are actually native to Central and South America, but they are often incorporated into island cuisine—there would hardly be a tropical culinary experience without them.

½ cup Dry Jamaican Jerk Spices (see recipe, page 137)

1½ tablespoons minced garlic

1 tablespoon minced jalapeño chile

¼ cup soy sauce

1 cup brown sugar

4½ cups pineapple juice

Zest of 1 lime (about ½ teaspoon)

¼ cup vegetable oil

Coarse salt

Freshly ground black pepper

2 three-pound racks of spare ribs

1 tablespoon dark chili powder

1 Scotch bonnet or habanero chile, cut in half

Preheat the oven to 250°F. Blend the jerk spices, garlic, jalapeño, soy sauce, ½ cup brown sugar, 4 cups pineapple juice, lime zest, oil, and salt and black pepper to taste in a small food processor. Season ribs with salt and pepper to taste, and rub generously with mixture. Place ribs in a baking pan; transfer to oven and cook 3 hours. Meanwhile, place the remaining 1 cup brown sugar, the remaining ½ cup pineapple juice, chili powder, and Scotch bonnet chile in a saucepan and cook until liquid is reduced by half.

Increase the oven temperature to 425°F or preheat the outdoor grill. Baste the ribs with the pineapple glaze, and continuing cooking 30 minutes, basting every 10 minutes, until meat is tender and pulls away from the bones. Slice racks into individual ribs; serve four, arranged crisscrossed, per person.

trinidadian beef pastelles in banana leaves

Makes 24 pastelles

Pastelles look like small packages or parcels. This dish is similar to Mexican tamales in preparation. A tasty and spicy filling rests on top of a pillow of corn dough. They are a special treat that is good for Mardi Gras or New Year's Eve. The banana leaves, which can be found in most Asian or Latino markets, impart a pleasantly subtle flavor.

4 cups cornmeal
2 tablespoons sugar
3 tablespoons coarse salt
2 tablespoons unsalted butter
8 cups boiling water
5 pounds beef round, cut into 1-inch cubes
1½ quarts beef stock
1½ cups finely chopped onion
¼ cup minced garlic
⅓ cup finely chopped jalapeño chile, seeded
1 red bell pepper, seeded, cored, and
   finely chopped
1 bunch thyme, chopped
½ cup packed chopped basil leaves
¼ cup capers
1½ cups currants
¼ cup chopped green olives
2 tablespoons ketchup
2½ tablespoons red-wine vinegar
⅓ cup maple syrup

¼ cup canned chipotle chiles, blended to puree
1 teaspoon freshly ground black pepper
4 whole banana leaves
½ cup vegetable oil, for brushing
12 grilled or broiled pineapple wedges,
   for garnish
New Soul Hot-Red-Pepper Sauce
   (see recipe, page 138)

In a large bowl, add cornmeal, sugar, 2 table-spoons salt, and butter. Slowly add the boiling water, and stir; the mixture should be moist enough to spread.

Preheat the oven to 350°F. Place beef in a roasting pan with stock, onions, garlic, and jalapeño. Cook 2 hours, or until beef is tender and pulls apart easily. Add red bell pepper, thyme, basil, capers, currants, olives, ketchup, red-wine vinegar, maple syrup, chilpotles, the remaining 1 tablespoon salt, and black pepper; cook an additional 20 minutes. Strain and shred beef with a fork. Taste and adjust seasoning if necessary.

Increase the oven to 425°F. Wash banana leaves, and cut into 8-inch squares. Brush each square with vegetable oil. Spread 1 tablespoon of corn dough on each, and top with 1½ tablespoons of the beef mixture. Fold in sides of the square toward the center, and then fold the tops underneath to create a secure square package. Place pastelles on a rack on top of a jelly-roll pan, and add ½ inch boiling water to pan. Bake 45 minutes, or until dough is firm. (You will need to open a pastelle to test the texture.)

Garnish with grilled or broiled pineapple wedges, and serve with New Soul Hot Red-Pepper Sauce.

ENTRÉES, main courses, BIG PLATES, dinner

Big plates are what traditional soul cuisine is all about. Over the years, main courses were simple and ordinarily ladled from a single pot. Today, we usually prepare vegetables and side dishes separately from our meats or fish. I serve individual portions and embellish the presentation with garnishes and side dishes as we do in restaurants, to keep the visual aspect appealing and exciting: give your guests something delicious not only to taste and smell but also to see.

filé-crusted scallops
with tomato and okra ragoût

Makes 4 servings

This dish is gumbo deconstructed. I've taken some of the components of a tradi-tional gumbo and created a lighter version using simple techniques. Sautéing—from the French verb *sauter,* meaning "to jump"—is an easy cooking method using high heat that makes the ingredients seem to leap from the pan. Okra has a dubious reputation because of its viscid texture when cooked, but in this preparation it retains the delicious crunch.

20 sea scallops (about 1½ pounds)
1 teaspoon filé powder
¼ teaspoon paprika
¼ teaspoon garlic powder
¼ teaspoon onion powder
Pinch cayenne pepper
⅓ cup extra-virgin olive oil
1 cup diced onions
2 cloves garlic
1½ cups cherry tomatoes, sliced in half
2 cups fresh okra, chopped into ½-inch pieces
½ teaspoon coarse salt, plus more to taste
¼ teaspoon freshly ground white pepper,
plus more to taste
2 tablespoons canola oil
1 bunch watercress or other salad green
1 tablespoon red-wine vinegar

Preheat the oven to 350°F. Remove and discard muscle attachment from scallops; rinse scallops and set aside. Mix filé powder, paprika, garlic and onion powders, and cayenne to create spice blend; set aside. Heat a large skillet over medium heat. Add 2 tablespoons olive oil, onions, and garlic, and cook until soft, about 10 minutes. Add tomato halves and cook 5 minutes, or until they begin to break apart. Add okra and season with ½ teaspoon salt, ¼ teaspoon white pepper, and 1 teaspoon spice blend. Reduce heat to low, and let mixture cook an additional 10 minutes.

Season reserved scallops with salt and white pepper. Dip one side of scallops into spice blend. Heat a large skillet with oven-proof handle over high heat, and add canola oil. Add scallops to pan with spice side down, and cook 2 minutes. Using a narrow spatula, turn scallops, and cook an additional 2 minutes. Transfer skillet to oven, and cook scallops an additional 3 minutes to ensure scallops are cooked through.

To serve Divide okra mixture among 4 plates, placing 3 piles of the mixture in each; arrange 4 scallops around the dish, and 1 in the center. Toss watercress with vinegar and remaining olive oil, and season with salt and white pepper to taste. Place greens on top of scallop in the center.

steamed lobster in gumbo z'herbes sauce

Makes 4 servings

Gumbo is actually a derivation of the African word for okra, the common ingredient found in most recipes, and the name reveals its origins. Gumbo as we know it is a thick stew—with a base of tomatoes, greens, and/or stock thickened with a roux—that is laden with chicken, sausage, and seafood. The New Soul version highlights sumptuous lobster.

2 three-pound lobsters
3 tablespoons vegetable oil
1 onion, diced
2 shallots, minced
3 cloves garlic, minced
1 jalapeño chile, seeded and finely chopped
½ pound fresh spinach
1 pound fresh kale
2 cups vegetable stock, fish stock, or
    clam juice
1 can (14 ounces) coconut milk
1½ cups water
1 pound fresh or frozen okra, cut into
    ¼-inch pieces
1 tablespoon filé powder
1 tablespoon chopped fresh thyme
1 pound Yukon gold or other yellow potatoes,
    diced small
Coarse salt
Freshly ground black pepper
Lemon slices, for garnish

In a large pot, bring 2 quarts water to a boil. Add lobsters and cook 8 minutes, remove and cool. When lobsters are cool, cut in half. Set aside.

In another clean, large pot, add vegetable oil and cook onion, shallots, garlic, and jalapeño over medium heat until soft, about 7 minutes. Add spinach, kale, stock, coconut milk, and the water; simmer 10 minutes. Remove greens and 1 cup liquid, and puree in a blender or food processor. Return greens mixture to pot, and add okra, filé powder, thyme, and potatoes. Continue cooking 20 minutes, and adjust seasoning with salt and pepper to taste.

To serve Ladle 1 cup gumbo sauce into each of 4 shallow bowls. Place ½ lobster tail and 1 claw in each bowl. Garnish with lemon slices.

creole marinated striped bass

Makes 4 servings

The flavors of peppers and onions dominate Creole cooking in Louisiana, and lend to a signature spicy and mouthwatering experience that many associate with the food of New Orleans. Here, striped bass—a flavorful fish by itself—is enhanced with the Creole tastes in this simple marinade, and the dish is a great example of a New Soul recipe with lots of flavor and no fat. The Roasted Corn Relish on page 145 is a wonderful accompaniment for this main course.

2 yellow onions, thinly sliced
4 cloves garlic, minced
2 tablespoons olive oil
1 teaspoon tomato paste
2 dashes hot-pepper sauce
2 dashes Worcestershire sauce
2 teaspoons chopped thyme
1 teaspoon chili powder
1 teaspoon sugar
Coarse salt
Freshly ground white pepper
1½ pounds striped bass fillet
Vegetable oil

Whisk together onions, garlic, olive oil, tomato paste, hot sauce, Worcestershire sauce, thyme, chili powder, sugar, and salt and white pepper to taste. Pour half of mixture into a small bowl, and set aside. Cut the fish into 4 equal portions, and place in shallow baking dish. Pour the remaining marinade over fish. Transfer to the refrigerator, and allow fish to marinate in refrigerator at least 4 hours, up to overnight. Preheat grill and brush lightly with vegetable oil. Remove fish from marinade, and grill approximately 4 minutes on each side, until the flesh of the fish is opaque and flaky, but not dry. Warm the reserved marinade, and pour over the cooked fish.

north african spiced salmon

Makes 4 servings

This spice mixture originated in Tunisia, but a good friend of mine from Algeria tells me that she grew up using it on everything from couscous to vegetables to meats. The rich flavor of salmon stands up to the assertive flavors of the spices, and your guests will be able to smell its exotic fragrance before they enter the dining room. Serving the salmon medium-rare to medium will emphasize its taste and texture. The Green Chile Harissa Sauce on page 147 is the best complement to this dish.

2 tablespoons grapeseed oil
4 six-ounce salmon fillets, skin removed
Coarse salt
4 tablespoons Ras el Hanout (recipe follows)

Heat oil in skillet. Season fish with salt to taste and roll in spice mixture just enough to lightly coat fillets. Cook, skin side up, over medium high heat 3 minutes; turn and cook an additional 3 minutes for medium rare.

RAS EL HANOUT
Makes about 1½ cups

This spice rub can be stored at room temperature in an airtight jar up to six months.

8 tablespoons black peppercorns
6 tablespoons toasted coriander seeds
6 tablespoons turmeric
4 tablespoons whole allspice
4 tablespoons ground cardamom
4 tablespoons ground cinnamon
4 tablespoons toasted cumin seeds
2 tablespoons cayenne pepper
2 tablespoons ground cloves
2 tablespoons ground ginger
2 tablespoons ground mace
2 tablespoons ground nutmeg
2 tablespoons dried thyme
5 bay leaves

Combine all ingredients, and grind in an electric spice/coffee grinder or with a mortar and pestle.

benne-crusted mahi mahi

with gingered cucumber relish

Makes 4 servings

Benne is the African word for sesame seeds, and their use is common in baked goods in Georgia and the Carolinas, where many Africans were brought to cultivate rice and other crops. I embellish the soul-food tradition by adding benne's superb crunchy texture and nutty flavor to the meaty Mahi Mahi.

4 six-ounce Mahi Mahi fillets
Coarse salt
Freshly ground white pepper
⅓ cup sesame seeds
2 tablespoons grapeseed oil
Gingered Cucumber Relish (recipe follows)

Preheat the oven to 350°F. Season the fish with salt and pepper to taste, and then roll in sesame seeds. Heat an ovenproof skillet over medium-high heat, and add grapeseed oil. Add fish and cook 3 minutes on each side to toast sesame seeds. Transfer fish to oven and cook through, about 3 minutes. Transfer to plates, and top each fillet with ½ cup relish.

GINGERED CUCUMBER RELISH
Makes about 2½ cups

2 cups cucumbers, pared, seeded, and diced
1 cup chopped green onions
1 piece (¼ inch) fresh ginger, minced
¼ teaspoon minced garlic
1 tablespoon freshly squeezed lemon juice
1 tablespoon sesame oil
1 tablespoon canola oil
1 tablespoon sugar
1 tablespoon rice-wine vinegar
¼ cup chopped cilantro leaves
1½ teaspoons chopped fresh red chiles
Coarse salt, to taste
Freshly ground white pepper, to taste

Place all ingredients together in a large bowl. Stir to combine.

pan-roasted halibut

with roasted beet tapenade

Makes 4 servings

The olive trees found in the south of France inspire many of my New Soul dishes, one of which is tapenade, a delicious spread made from olives, fresh herbs, and spices. It is typically served with a big plate of vegetables, but, with its salty and lemony components, it's also the ideal condiment for fish. I've substituted roasted beets—the roasting brings out the natural sweetness of the root vegetable—to create a new color and flavor blend. I prefer to use Pacific halibut to avoid varieties that are overfished.

1 pound beets
4 tablespoons vegetable oil
Coarse salt
Freshly ground white pepper
1 teaspoon anchovy paste
2 teaspoons capers
1 tablespoon chopped thyme
1 tablespoon chopped parsley
1 teaspoon minced garlic
1 tablespoon freshly squeezed lemon juice
2 tablespoons extra-virgin olive oil
Pinch cayenne pepper
1½ pounds halibut fillet, cut into 4 equal
   portions

Preheat the oven to 350°F. Trim and wash beets. Place beets in a roasting pan and toss with 2 tablespoons vegetable oil, and a sprinkle of salt and white pepper. Cover with foil and roast about 1 hour, or until a paring knife penetrates the flesh easily, depending on size of beets. Peel beets by rubbing away skin with a paper towel. Cut beets into small dice; place in a medium bowl and toss with anchovy paste, capers, thyme, parsley, garlic, lemon juice, olive oil, and cayenne. Place half of the beet mixture into a food processor, and process until smooth. Return the mixture to bowl, and season to taste with salt and white pepper.

Heat an ovenproof skillet over medium-high heat, and add remaining vegetable oil. Season fish with salt and white pepper, and add fish to pan with skin side up. Cook 4 to 5 minutes, until well browned. Turn fish; transfer skillet to oven, and cook 3 minutes, or until cooked through.

black cod in crab boil broth

Makes 4 servings

A traditional crab boil involves cooking numerous crabs in a flavorful broth with corn, potatoes, and sausages. The broth also makes a great poaching liquid for many varieties of fish and shellfish. This is a fabulous summertime one-pot meal when the sweetest, best-tasting corn is available.

4 cups water
2 cups clam juice
Crab-Boil Mix (recipe follows)
1½ tablespoons yellow mustard seeds
2 bay leaves
½ teaspoon coarse salt
1 tablespoon minced garlic
½ cup minced onion
1 cup canned diced tomatoes
1 tablespoon fresh thyme leaves
½ pound andouille (or other spicy sausage), sliced
1 pound red bliss potatoes, scrubbed and cut into bite-sized pieces
2 ears corn on the cob, shucked
1½ pounds black cod or other firm white fish
Fresh chopped parsley for garnish

In a large pot, bring the water and clam juice to a boil. Add Crab-Boil Mix, mustard seeds, bay leaves, and salt; return to a boil. Add garlic, onions, tomatoes, thyme, sausage, and potatoes; reduce to a simmer, and cook 10 minutes. Add corn, and cook an additional 10 minutes.

Remove corn, and let it cool slightly; cut kernels from the cob, leaving most of the pieces in large chunks. Return the corn to the pot. Add fish and cook over medium heat until cooked through. The flesh should be flaky but still hold together. Add parsley and serve in a shallow bowl.

CRAB-BOIL MIX

1 teaspoon black peppercorns
½ teaspoon celery seeds
½ teaspoon coriander seeds
½ teaspoon crushed red pepper
½ teaspoon ground ginger
⅛ teaspoon ground mace
1 lemon, cut in half

Place peppercorns, celery seeds, and coriander seeds in a spice grinder; pulse several times. Transfer mixture to a small bowl, and add crushed pepper, ginger, and mace; mix well. Spoon half of the dry mixture over each lemon half. Then place each lemon half in a 4-inch square of cheese-cloth. Tie each cheesecloth into a bundle with kitchen twine.

blackened tilapia

Makes 4 servings

Blackened dishes are always equated with Louisiana Creole cooking. The spices can be used on meat, poultry, fish, and even tofu. The key to the blackening is to use a heavy skillet that can take the requisite high heat. The Piccalilli Julienne is a classic Southern relish that combines the sweet and the sour and offers a cooling relief and refreshing contrast to the spicy blackening mixture. Serve this dish with mounds of steaming hot white rice.

2 tablespoons coarse salt
3 tablespoons paprika
2 tablespoons garlic powder
2 tablespoons onion powder
1 tablespoon cayenne pepper
1 tablespoon freshly ground black pepper
1 tablespoon dried oregano
1 tablespoon dried thyme
4 six-ounce tilapia fillets
3 tablespoons canola oil
Piccalilli Julienne (see recipe, page 142)

In a shallow dish, mix the salt, paprika, garlic and onion powders, cayenne, black pepper, oregano, and thyme. Generously coat fish filets with spice mixture. Heat a large cast-iron skillet over medium-high heat, and add canola oil. Add fish and cook 3 minutes on each side, or until flesh is white opaque (cooked through) and spices are toasted. Transfer to plates, and serve each fillet with ½ cup Piccalilli Julienne.

cornmeal-battered trout

Makes 4 servings

Fish fry suppers are a classic soul food specialty. Typically, the fish is deep-fried whole, but I've opted for a more user-friendly version. For a delicious tartar sauce to accompany this fish, pulse Piccalilli Julienne on page 142 with mayonnaise and green Tabasco sauce.

1 large egg
1 cup water
¾ cup flour
½ cup cornmeal
1 tablespoon chopped parsley
½ teaspoon garlic powder
½ teaspoon onion powder
1 teaspoon salt
¼ teaspoon freshly ground white pepper
2 rainbow or brook trout, head removed and butterflied
½ cup canola oil
Lemon wedges, for garnish

Mix egg and the water, and slowly whisk in flour and cornmeal. Add parsley, garlic and onion powders, salt, and white pepper. Lay prepared fish in batter.

In heavy skillet (preferably cast iron or nonstick), heat oil over medium-high heat. Fry fish 3 minutes on each side. Remove and drain on paper towels. Squeeze lemon over fish and garnish with lemon slices.

molasses-barbecued chicken

Makes 4 servings

There must be over one thousand versions of barbecue sauce across the United States, and there are many secret recipes—here I'm gladly sharing my favorite. The molasses gives the sauce an intense and distinctive flavor, and cooking the chicken over a medium flame will help to prevent the sugar in the molasses from burning. This sauce works just as well on ribs, steak, and even salmon.

4 tablespoons unsalted butter

4 red onions, minced

¼ cup minced garlic

1 piece (3 inches) fresh ginger, minced

¼ cup Dijon-style mustard

1 cup cider vinegar

½ cup soy sauce

½ cup ketchup

⅓ cup Worcestershire sauce

¼ cup freshly squeezed lemon juice

2 cups dark-brown sugar

¼ cup chipotle chiles in adobo, blended
   into puree

3 tablespoons dark chili powder

2 cans (28 ounces each) peeled,
   chopped plum tomatoes

1 cup molasses

Coarse salt

Freshly ground black pepper

1 large chicken (3½ pounds), cut into pieces

In a large pot, melt butter and add onions, garlic, and ginger. Cook 10 minutes, or until soft, and then add mustard, vinegar, soy sauce, ketchup, Worcestershire sauce, lemon juice, brown sugar, chile puree, and chili powder. Cook over medium heat for an additional 10 minutes. Add tomatoes and molasses, and cook 30 minutes. Season to taste with salt and pepper.

Preheat the grill or broiler. Season chicken with salt and pepper to taste, and generously coat with barbecue sauce. Cook chicken 4 minutes on each side, then move chicken away from flame, and continue to grill until cooked through, about 15 minutes. Store the remaining barbecue sauce in an airtight jar in refrigerator for up to 1 month.

yassa chicken with carrots and leeks

Makes 4 to 6 servings

Yassa chicken is a classic dish of Senegal, a French-speaking country in West Africa. This dish is at once tangy and spicy. Typically it is a humble one-pot dish, but here I've updated it for the New Soul kitchen by adding julienned vegetables— such as leeks, carrots, red peppers, and celery—and fresh lime zest. Serve the chicken with white rice and sautéed greens.

2 limes
1½ cups thinly sliced onions
6 cloves garlic, halved
1 cup thinly sliced celery (about 2 ribs)
1 cup thinly sliced carrots
1 fresh hot chile pepper (Scotch bonnet or habanero), quartered
1 large chicken (3 to 3½ pounds), cut into 8 pieces
1 teaspoon coarse salt, plus more for seasoning
Freshly ground black pepper
2 tablespoons vegetable oil
1 quart chicken stock
2 cups julienned leeks
2 cups julienned carrots
½ cup water
1 tablespoon unsalted butter

Remove the zest from the limes and reserve; juice limes to yield about ½ cup. Place lime juice, onions, garlic, celery, sliced carrots, and chile into a bowl, and combine. Place chicken in mixture, and marinate 3 to 5 hours. Strain and discard liquid. Remove the chicken, and reserve the vegetables. Pat chicken dry with paper towels, and season with salt and pepper to taste.

Heat a Dutch oven over medium-high heat, and add vegetable oil. Transfer chicken to Dutch oven and brown, about 5 minutes. Remove chicken and set aside; skim off excess fat from Dutch oven.

Preheat the oven to 250°F. Add chicken stock to Dutch oven, and scrape the bottom to loosen any meaty bits. Add chicken and marinated vegetables. Continue cooking, covered, over medium heat until chicken is tender, about 30 minutes. Remove chicken and place on baking sheet; transfer to oven to keep warm. Strain the sauce through sieve or cone-shaped strainer. Season the sauce with reserved lime zest, salt, and pepper. Remove chicken, and spoon sauce over. Keep chicken warm until serving.

Bring a pot of water to a boil, and then add 1 teaspoon salt. Add leeks to pot, and cook until soft, about 1 minute. Remove leeks with slotted spoon, and place in ice water to stop cooking; drain. Repeat process with carrots. Before serving the chicken, warm the blanched carrots and leeks in water and butter, plus salt and pepper to taste. Garnish with the vegetables.

pecan-crusted boneless chicken breasts with roasted garlic gravy

Makes 4 servings

The often-insipid boneless chicken breast is made exciting with this crunchy and spicy coating of pecan mixture. This dish also features one of my favorite flavor enhancers: roasted garlic. When roasted, garlic becomes a thick, sweet paste with a more complex flavor than when raw. When you're busy, this is a quick and easy way to experience lots of flavor for a minimal amount of effort.

1½ cups all-purpose flour
2 teaspoons freshly ground white pepper
1 tablespoon coarse salt
2 large eggs
2 tablespoons milk
1½ cups pecan pieces
1½ teaspoons crushed red pepper
2 pounds boneless and skinless chicken
   breasts
½ cup vegetable oil
Roasted Garlic Gravy (recipe follows)

Preheat the oven to 350°F. Have ready three shallow dishes or pans. In a small bowl, mix together the flour, white pepper, and salt, and transfer to the first dish. Whisk together eggs and milk, and transfer to the second dish. Using a food processor, grind together pecans, crushed red pepper, and 2 tablespoons of flour mixture, and transfer to the third dish.

Dredge chicken breasts in the flour mixture. Shake off excess; dip into the egg mixture, and then roll in the pecan crust.

In a large skillet, heat oil over medium heat, add coated chicken breasts, and cook 3 minutes on each side, or until pecans are lightly toasted. Remove chicken breasts from skillet; do not pour out oil because you will use it to make the gravy. Transfer chicken to a baking dish. Place dish in oven, and continue to cook chicken 6 minutes, or until cooked through. Serve with Roasted Garlic Gravy.

ROASTED GARLIC GRAVY
Makes about 1½ cups

¾ cup minced onions
½ cup white wine
1½ cups chicken stock
1½ tablespoons roasted garlic
   (see instructions, page 98)
Coarse salt
Freshly ground white pepper

DIscard most of the oil from the skillet used to cook chicken, and then add the minced onions. Cook onions over medium heat until soft, about 5 minutes, and add wine. Cook until most of wine has evaporated. Add chicken stock, and whisk in roasted garlic. Reduce heat to low, and cook sauce over low heat an additional 5 minutes, strain, and season to taste with salt and pepper.

brazilian-spiced oven-roasted chicken

Makes 4 servings

This delicious crisp-roasted chicken is made transcendent by a combination of fresh citrus zest, hot chiles, and fragrant spice. Brazil has the largest population of people of African descent in the Western Hemisphere, and this fact is largely reflected in its cuisine of spicy foods that incorporate chiles, paprika, and copious amounts of garlic.

2 tablespoons minced jalapeño chile
   (about 1 large chile)
1½ tablespoons minced garlic
1 tablespoon coarse salt
1 teaspoon paprika
1 teaspoon turmeric
1 teaspoon freshly ground black pepper
Zest of 1 orange (about 1 tablespoon)
Zest of 2 lemons (about 1 tablespoon)
½ cup coconut milk
1 large (3½ pound) chicken

Preheat the oven to 425°F. Combine jalapeño, garlic, salt, paprika, turmeric, black pepper, zests, and coconut milk to form a paste. Rub chicken skin and inner cavity with spice paste. Tie chicken to secure legs. Bake in a roasting pan for 25 minutes to crisp skin; reduce oven to 350°F, and bake for an additional 30 minutes, or until juices run clear. Serve with side dish of your choice.

groundnut, chicken, and cabbage stew

Makes 6 servings

This stew is the perfect treat for the grown-up peanut butter lover because of its comfortingly familiar taste combined with nutritional vegetables. Groundnut is a traditional name for the peanut because of the way that it grows on a vine that buries its pods into the ground. It's not a nut, however—it's a legume. Peanut butter naturally thickens this stew and adds a rich and unusual flavor. Other vegetables such as eggplant, okra, sweet potatoes, turnips, and bell peppers make this dish sublime. Serve the stew over hot rice.

2 tablespoons vegetable or peanut oil
1 large chicken (3 to 3½ pounds), cut into
    8 pieces
Coarse salt
Freshly ground white pepper
1 tablespoon unsalted butter
2 onions, diced small
5 carrots, sliced diagonally ¼-inch thick
1 head green cabbage, cut into 8 pieces
    and then halved
4 cloves garlic, mashed
1 piece (1 inch) fresh ginger, peeled and sliced
1½ cups chopped tomatoes
6 cups chicken stock or broth, heated
1 tablespoon fresh thyme leaves, chopped
1 habanero (or Scotch bonnet) chile pepper,
    pierced
1 cup smooth natural peanut butter
2 tablespoons tomato paste
½ cup roasted, unsalted peanuts, chopped,
    for garnish

Heat oil in a Dutch oven set over medium-high heat. Season chicken pieces with salt and pepper to taste, and then brown in hot pan; set aside. Drain off excess fat. Add butter, and cook onions 5 minutes, or until soft.

Add carrots, cabbage, garlic, ginger, and chopped tomatoes to the Dutch oven. Add 4 cups of hot chicken stock, thyme, and habanero. Whisk in peanut butter and tomato paste into remaining stock, and then add chicken back to pan. Bring to a boil, and then simmer for 2 to 2½ hours, or until chicken falls from bones. Season to taste with salt and pepper. Garnish with chopped peanuts.

mustard barbecued cornish game hens

Makes 4 servings

Mustard barbecue sauces are usually reserved for pulled pork, but they also work well with a dense piece of poultry. Quail can replace the cornish game hens in this recipe. However, many cooks may not have access to these tiny little birds. The smaller quail will cook more quickly, so adjust the cooking time accordingly. Add a side of coleslaw or some sautéed greens to make this into a rounded, satisfying meal.

1 cup minced onions
4 cloves garlic, minced
1 tablespoon unsalted butter
½ cup cider vinegar
2 teaspoons dry mustard
3 teaspoons yellow mustard seeds
¼ teaspoon cayenne pepper
½ cup granulated sugar
2 teaspoons Worcestershire sauce
¼ teaspoon garlic powder
½ teaspoon onion powder
1 tablespoon honey
1 teaspoon crushed red pepper
¼ teaspoon turmeric
2 lemons, juiced
Coarse salt
Freshly ground white pepper
2 Cornish game hens

Preheat the oven to 350°F. In a medium saucepan, cook onions and garlic in butter until soft and translucent, and then add vinegar, dry mustard, mustard seeds, cayenne, sugar, Worcestershire sauce, garlic and onion powders, honey, crushed red pepper, turmeric, lemon juice, and salt and pepper to taste. Cook 15 minutes, or until the mixture resembles a paste. Generously baste hens with mustard sauce. Cook on a rack placed inside a roasting pan for about 1 hour, or until juices run clear.

buttermilk and sage–soaked turkey breast

Makes 6 servings

There can't be a simpler recipe than this to greatly impart flavor to a sometimes otherwise lackluster piece of turkey. When you're in the mood for Thanksgiving flavor and not yet ready for the commitment of roasting an entire turkey, this dish provides a tantalizing alternative. The acid in the buttermilk tenderizes the meat of the breast as it marinates overnight: the lactose caramelizes on the skin under the high heat in the beginning of the cooking process, and the garlic slivers caramelize as the turkey breast continues to cook.

1 three-pound turkey breast with bone
¼ cup chopped sage leaves
4 cloves garlic, sliced thin
1 tablespoon coarse salt
Freshly ground white pepper, to taste
½ teaspoon onion granules
2 cups buttermilk

Rub the turkey breast with sage and garlic, tucking pieces of each underneath any pieces of skin. Place the turkey breast in a small roasting pan. Whisk salt, white pepper, and onion granules into buttermilk, and pour the mixture over turkey breast. Marinate the turkey in the refrigerator overnight, up to 24 hours.

Preheat the oven to 425°F. Drain off liquid from turkey marinade, and cook turkey breast 45 minutes to crisp skin. Reduce heat to 350°F and cook until the turkey breast reaches an internal temperature of 170°F on a meat thermometer, about 1 hour.

hot pepper and citrus–rubbed skirt steak

Makes 4 servings

This rub mixture has an evocative island flavor that is perfect for a summer grilling party or an inspired middle-of-winter dish. You'll be amazed at how far a little citrus zest will go to enhance the taste. The skirt steak is becoming an increasingly popular cut of meat. It's marbled with a small amount of fat and thus naturally flavorful, and it's reasonably priced.

2 red hot chiles (such as Thai), seeds and membranes removed
2 green hot chiles (such as jalapeño or serrano), seeds and membranes removed
Zest of 1 lemon
Zest of 1 lime
Zest of 1 orange
4 cloves garlic
2 tablespoons fresh chopped cilantro leaves
¼ teaspoon ground cumin
½ teaspoon freshly ground black pepper
1 tablespoon honey
1½ tablespoons olive oil
2 pounds skirt steak (or flank steak)
Coarse salt

Place chiles, zests, garlic, cilantro, cumin, black pepper, honey, and olive oil in a food processor; pulse to blend. Generously rub meat with chile mixture and transfer to refrigerator to chill 2 hours. Preheat broiler or grill. Season meat with salt to taste, and cook to desired doneness, 2½ to 3 minutes on each side for medium-rare.

lamb chops with brandied peach chutney

Makes 4 servings

Southerners adopted chutneys from the East Indians and have reinvented this specialty many times. My aunt Essie tells me that my grandfather Mac Thomas was a big fan of peach brandy. He had a peach tree in the backyard and often experimented to create his special blend. I wanted to take that recipe a step further—here, juicy summer peaches, peppers, onions, and spices become a luscious accompaniment for grilled lamb chops in no time at all. The precise cooking time depends on the thickness of your cut of meat, so don't hesitate to ask your butcher to suggest a cooking time.

4 large lamb loin chops or 8 rib lamb chops
Coarse salt
Freshly ground black pepper
Brandied Peach Chutney (recipe follows)

Heat a large skillet over medium-high heat. Season lamb with salt and a generous amount of pepper. Add lamb to skillet, and cook on both sides to desired doneness. Serve with Brandied Peach Chutney.

BRANDIED PEACH CHUTNEY
Makes about 2 cups

This chutney can be made up to two days in advance and will keep up to one week, refrigerated, in an airtight container.

1½ pounds fresh peaches (or about 4 large peaches)
½ cup brandy
1 cup freshly squeezed orange juice
Zest of 1 orange
1 large green bell pepper, cored, seeded, and diced
2 red onions, diced
¾ cup brown sugar
1½ tablespoons minced jalapeño chile

2 cloves garlic, minced

1 piece (2 inches) fresh ginger, grated

2 teaspoons yellow mustard seeds

1 teaspoon whole coriander seeds, toasted
  and crushed

½ teaspoon coarse salt

¼ teaspoon ground allspice

¼ teaspoon ground white pepper

2 cinnamon sticks

1 bay leaf

Bring a large pot of water to a boil. Cut an X into
the end of the peach opposite of the stem. Place
peaches in boiling water until skins begin to pull
away from flesh. Remove peaches and plunge
them into a bowl of ice water to stop the cooking.
Drain and peel peaches, and chop into small dice.

In a medium saucepan over medium-high heat,
add brandy, orange juice, zest, bell pepper,
onions, brown sugar, jalapeño, garlic, ginger,
mustard and coriander seeds, salt, allspice,
white pepper, cinnamon sticks, and bay leaf;
stir to combine. Add the peaches, and cook
45 minutes, or until bell pepper and onion are
soft and most of the liquid has evaporated.
Remove bay leaf and cinnamon sticks.
Serve warm.

hickory and maple–glazed pork tenderloin with apple cider sauce

Makes 4 servings

Pork and apples is certainly one of the most perfect flavor combinations, and this slightly sweet apple-cider sauce beautifully enhances the taste of the hickory-smoked pork. It also reminds me of the country-fried apples we had at my grandmother Flora Holland's house, which were served at breakfast with sausage and ham. A tart variety of apples, such as Granny Smith, works best here.

2 tablespoons each thyme, sage, and
   rosemary, reserve stems for Apple Cider
   Sauce
4 eight-ounce pieces pork tenderloin
⅓ cup pure maple syrup
1 cup hickory or other fragrant wood
   smoking chips
Coarse salt
Freshly ground black pepper
Apple Cider Sauce (recipe follows)

Preheat grill. Pick herb leaves from stems. Roughly chop leaves (1), and combine in a small bowl. Roll pork in maple syrup and then rub with herbs (2); set aside. To smoke inside, place wood chips in a roasting pan (3), and place wire rack on top. Heat the baking sheet on a burner until the chips just begin to smoke. Place pork on wire rack, and cover with foil. Allow pork to smoke 15 minutes. Season with salt and black pepper to taste. Grill 6 to 7 minutes on both sides, until pork is cooked medium-well. Serve with Apple Cider Sauce.

APPLE CIDER SAUCE

Makes about 3 cups

Preparing this sauce in a nonreactive pot allows the sugar to reduce and become syrupy without evaporating. You can prepare this up to a week in advance. Allow it to cool and store in an airtight container in the refrigerator.

1 quart chicken stock
½ cup apple cider
¼ cup Madeira wine
¼ cup light-brown sugar
½ onion, quartered
2 cloves garlic
1 teaspoon whole black peppercorns
2 slices uncooked bacon
Stems of picked herbs used for pork
2 green apples, peeled, cored, and sliced thin

In a medium nonreactive pot, heat all ingredients except apples over medium heat, and reduce to 1 cup, about 20 minutes. Strain mixture, and discard solids. Add apples to the sauce, and continue to cook until apples are tender, about 15 minutes.

jamaican curried oxtail

Makes 4 servings

This dish reveals the East Indian influence in the West Indies. Curries are found throughout the Caribbean—from the typical curried goat in Jamaica all the way down to Trinidad, where shrimp curry is a specialty. The oxtail absorbs the flavor of the fragrant spice mixture and is incredibly tender and juicy when slowly simmered.

3 tablespoons canola oil

3 pounds oxtail

2 teaspoons coarse salt, plus more to taste

2 teaspoons freshly ground black pepper,
   plus more to taste

3 cloves garlic, minced (about 1½ tablespoons)

1 yellow onion, minced

3 green onions, chopped

1 red bell pepper, cored, seed, and diced

1½ tablespoons curry powder

¼ teaspoon turmeric

½ teaspoon ground cumin

½ teaspoon garam masala

½ teaspoon garlic granules

½ teaspoon celery seeds

1 tablespoon chopped thyme

3 tablespoons water

3 tablespoons vegetable oil

1 tablespoon tomato paste

1 quart beef broth

1 tablespoon cornstarch, dissolved in
   2 tablespoons water

1 cup coconut milk

2 Idaho potatoes, peeled and cubed

In a large pot, heat canola oil over medium heat. Lightly sprinkle oxtail with 1 teaspoon each of salt and black pepper and add to pot. Brown on both sides. Remove oxtail, and add garlic, onion, and bell pepper, and cook until soft, 5 to 6 minutes.

Combine 1 teaspoon salt, 1 teaspoon black pepper, spices, and thyme in a small bowl; mix with the water to make a smooth paste. Add spice paste and return oxtail to pot. Mix until oxtail and onion mixture are coated with spice paste; add tomato paste and beef broth. Bring to a boil, and then add dissolved cornstarch. Reduce heat to a simmer, and cook oxtail, covered, 1½ hours. Add coconut milk and potatoes; cook an additional 30 minutes, or until meat and potatoes are tender. Season to taste with salt and pepper.

cornmeal crêpes
with okra ratatouille

Makes 12 crêpes

Ratatouille, a thick tomato stew usually made with eggplant, is a popular side dish in the south of France, and this recipe is yet another dish that incorporates my French cooking experience into the New Soul kitchen. Okra's glutinous consistency, which is activated when it is cooked in a liquid, is what makes it so useful in African-influenced dishes—it's a natural thickening agent. The light cornmeal crêpes are a nicely textured accompaniment for a great first course or vegetarian main course.

2 large eggs
2 cups milk
1 cup cornmeal
1 cup flour
1 teaspoon baking powder
½ teaspoon sugar
½ teaspoon coarse salt
⅛ teaspoon freshly ground white pepper
1 tablespoon unsalted butter, melted
Vegetable spray
Okra Ratatouille (recipe follows)

In a large bowl whisk eggs, and add milk. In a smaller bowl sift together dry ingredients and slowly whisk into egg mixture. Add melted butter. Heat a crêpe pan or nonstick 8-inch skillet over medium heat, and spray with vegetable spray. Add 2 heaping tablespoons batter at once and swirl to cover the bottom of the pan. Cook crêpe 2 minutes, or until edges start to brown; flip crêpe and cook the other side, about 15 seconds, or until lightly browned. Transfer to a plate lined with waxed paper. Continue cooking crêpes until all batter is used, placing waxed paper between individual crêpes. Lay one crêpe on dinner plate. Scoop about ⅓ cup ratatouille on to a quarter of a section of the crêpe. Fold crêpe in half, and then fold the empty half over on top of a ratatouille-filled quarter. Serve immediately.

OKRA RATATOUILLE

Makes about 4 cups

Okra Ratatouille can be made two days in advance and keeps up to one week, refrigerated, in an airtight container.

3 small zucchini, diced
2 red bell peppers, cored, seeded, and diced
2 tablespoons olive oil
Coarse salt
Freshly ground black pepper
1 onion, diced
4 cloves garlic, minced
1 can (28 ounces) peeled, chopped tomatoes
2 teaspoons tomato paste
¼ teaspoon cayenne pepper
¼ cup chopped basil
2 teaspoons chopped thyme
1 tablespoon chopped parsley
½ pound fresh okra (about 16 to 18 pods)

Preheat the oven to 375°F. Roast zucchini and peppers in separate baking pans with 1 tablespoon olive oil and salt and pepper to taste 30 minutes. Meanwhile, in a large skillet over medium heat, add 1 tablespoon olive oil; cook onion and garlic 3 to 4 minutes, until soft and translucent. Add diced roasted vegetables, tomatoes, tomato paste, cayenne, and herbs. Cook 10 minutes; add okra, and season with salt and pepper to taste. Cook an additional 10 minutes, or until okra is tender but still crisp.

hominy, mushroom, and butternut squash stew

Makes 6 to 8 servings

This nourishing stew will warm you up on a cold winter afternoon and also awaken your taste buds. It's filled with hominy—a dried corn that is treated in such a way that it softens, swells, and whitens. It's the perfect match for fleshy fall and winter mushrooms and squash.

2 tablespoons unsalted butter

2 cups chopped leeks

1½ cups shiitake mushrooms, stemmed and chopped

½ pound cremini mushrooms, stemmed and chopped

2 tablespoons roasted garlic (see instructions, page 98)

2 quarts vegetable broth

2 tablespoons chopped fresh marjoram

½ butternut squash, peeled, halved, seeded, and cut into 1-inch pieces (about 4 cups)

1 can (30 ounces) hominy

1 pound kale, large stems removed and torn into 1-inch pieces

Coarse salt

Freshly ground white pepper

In a large pot over medium heat, add butter and leeks. Cook until leeks are soft, about 15 minutes. Stir in mushrooms and garlic. Cover with vegetable broth, and add marjoram, squash, and hominy. Cook until squash is fork-tender, and then add kale. Continue to cook until kale is wilted. Season with salt and pepper to taste.

seasonal squash jambalaya

Makes 8 servings

When most people hear "jambalaya," they think of a plate of seasoned seafood, ham, and rice. Some argue that the origin of the dish is Spanish paella; others say it's French inspired. Either way, it's the Creole and Cajun people of Louisiana who have made it famous. I wanted to create a delicious vegetarian version for my friends Erik and Rhonda Albert, proprietors of the Oak Bluffs Inn on Martha's Vineyard. The chayote, or mirliton, squash looks like a light-green avocado. In the West Indies, it is called a christophene—thick fleshed, firm, and with a delicate vegetal flavor. Almost any variety of squash can be used in this versatile recipe.

1 acorn squash
4 tablespoons vegetable oil
1 teaspoon coarse salt
½ teaspoon freshly ground black pepper,
  plus more to taste
1½ onions, minced
4 cloves garlic, minced
2 ribs celery, minced
1 red bell pepper, cored, seeded,
  and diced
1 green bell pepper, cored, seeded,
  and diced
1 jalapeño chile, minced
1 tablespoon tomato paste
1 can (14½ ounces) peeled, chopped
  tomatoes plus ½ can water

3 cups vegetable broth
1 chayote squash, peeled and diced
2 small zucchini, diced
1 pound sunburst or pattypan squash, diced
1 tablespoon chopped thyme
1 teaspoon chopped rosemary
1 teaspoon chopped tarragon
½ teaspoon chopped sage
½ teaspoon chopped oregano
2 bay leaves
½ teaspoon crushed red pepper
½ teaspoon paprika
1 tablespoon Worcestershire sauce
2 cups long-grain rice

Preheat the oven to 400°F. Peel acorn squash, cut in half, and remove seeds. Cut the acorn squash into a medium dice, and toss with 1 tablespoon vegetable oil, 1 teaspoon salt, and black pepper to taste; roast in a baking pan for 20 minutes.

In a large pot over medium heat, heat remaining vegetable oil, and add onions, garlic, celery, bell peppers, and jalapeño. Cook until vegetables are soft, and then add tomato paste, canned tomatoes and the ½ can water, and vegetable broth. Bring to a boil.

Add the chatoye, zucchini, sunburst squash, thyme, rosemary, tarragon, sage, oregano, bay leaves, crushed red pepper, ½ teaspoon black pepper, paprika, Worcestershire sauce, and rice to the pot. Cover, and cook 30 minutes. Serve immediately.

vegetable and red bean gumbo

Makes 6 servings

Classic gumbo ingredients—roux, filé powder, and okra—make the base for this hearty stew of mixed vegetables. Tofu, tempeh, or seitan can also be added for extra protein. Serve each portion with ½ cup white rice.

1 cup plus 3 tablespoons vegetable oil
1 cup all-purpose flour
1½ cups diced onions
1 cup diced celery
1½ cups diced red bell peppers
1½ cups diced green bell peppers
2 tablespoon minced garlic
6 cups vegetable broth or water
1 can (14½ ounces) peeled, chopped
  plum tomatoes
2 teaspoons filé powder
½ teaspoon paprika
½ teaspoon celery seeds
¼ teaspoon cayenne pepper
½ teaspoon freshly ground black pepper
2 bay leaves
1 tablespoon chopped thyme
2 tablespoons chopped parsley
¾ pound red kidney beans, soaked overnight
2 cups diced turnips (about 1 pound)
2½ cups fresh or frozen okra, cut into ½-inch
  pieces
Coarse salt to taste
Chopped green onions, for garnish

To make the roux, heat a large skillet over medium heat; add 1 cup vegetable oil and flour. Cook, whisking occasionally, until mixture is medium brown, 8 to 10 minutes. Set aside.

In a large pot, heat 3 tablespoons vegetable oil over medium heat. Add onions, celery, bell peppers, and garlic, and cook 15 minutes, or until vegetables are soft. Add vegetable broth, tomatoes, ½ cup roux, filé, paprika, celery seeds, cayenne, black pepper, bay leaves, thyme, and parsley. Bring to a boil, and add kidney beans. Cook 45 minutes, or until beans soften. Add turnips, okra, and salt; cook an additional 30 minutes. If desired, add more roux for thicker gumbo. Adjust seasonings if necessary. Garnish with chopped green onions.

african peanut and root vegetable stew

Makes 6 to 8 servings

Peanuts and peanut butter are such favorite simple foods in this country that many of us don't think to use them as part of a recipe. In Asia and Africa, the peanut and peanut butter are commonly used as flavorings, thickeners, and are important ingredients in many savory dishes. The use of the peanut and its by-products can be traced back to Africa in the fifteenth century; this legume is clearly an important contribution to American cuisine.

2 tablespoons peanut or vegetable oil
2 cups diced white onions
¼ cup minced garlic
1 piece (3 inches) fresh ginger, minced
1 tablespoon cumin seeds
2 teaspoons coriander seeds
3 small red hot chiles (such as Thai), chopped
2 cups peeled, seeded and chopped plum tomatoes
1 teaspoon whole white peppercorns
1 teaspoon ground turmeric
1½ cups dry sherry
8 cups vegetable broth
1½ cups coconut milk
1 cup smooth natural peanut butter
2 cups peeled and diced turnips
2 cups peeled and diced carrots
2 cups peeled and diced sweet potatoes
Coarse salt
Freshly ground white pepper

In a large pot over low to medium heat, heat oil. Cook onions, garlic, and ginger 10 minutes, or until onions are translucent.

Meanwhile, toast cumin and coriander seeds in a small skillet over medium heat 3 minutes, or until lightly brown and fragrant. Let cool. Add chiles and tomatoes to onion mixture. In a spice grinder, grind cumin and coriander seeds with white peppercorns. Add ground seeds and turmeric to onion mixture. Cook, stirring, 2 minutes; add sherry. Cook until most of the sherry has evaporated, about 5 minutes.

Add vegetable broth and coconut milk. Blend with an immersion blender; alternatively, let cool slightly and transfer in small batches to a blender and blend. Strain through a sieve with medium holes (not mesh). Return to pot, and whisk in peanut butter. Add turnips, carrots, and sweet potatoes. Cook until vegetables are soft to the bite, but not mushy. Season to taste with salt and white pepper.

sides...

SIDES...

sides

In both traditional and New Soul cooking, delicious side dishes are necessary to round out a meal. These range from lightly seasoned fresh vegetables to baked gratins. When I was growing up, our dinner guests often brought a side to complement the main course. This took a lot of pressure off my parents whenever they anticipated a big crowd. Here, I share dishes that range from rice pilaf to sweet potatoes rösti. The only recipe that I find difficult to reinterpret, which I mention here to emphasize tradition, is the ubiquitous macaroni and cheese. Most of these sides can be served buffet style, but I've included suggestions for some of the main dishes they best complement.

peppered gruyère baked grits

Makes 6 servings

Head anywhere below the Mason-Dixon Line, and you'll find grits are one of the most popular starch side dishes, served at every meal. I've added a pungent, aged cheese and freshly ground black pepper. These grits pair particularly well with the Hot Pepper and Citrus-Rubbed Flank Steak on page 65.

4 cups water
1 teaspoon coarse salt
1 cup instant grits
½ teaspoon coarsely ground black pepper
3 cups shredded Gruyère cheese
2 tablespoons unsalted butter
Freshly grated nutmeg, to taste

Preheat the oven to 350°F. In a small saucepan, bring the water to a boil, and then add the salt and grits. Cook 5 to 7 minutes, stirring constantly, until grits are fully cooked but not dry. Stir in pepper, cheese, butter, and nutmeg, and transfer mixture to a 1½ quart baking dish. Bake 30 minutes until brown and bubbly on top.

basmati rice and three-pea pilaf

Makes 8 servings

The best things about a pilaf are the textures and colors that vary to create something that is at once beautiful and delicious. Basmati rice is the fragrant long-grain variety often associated with East Indian cuisine, but here I use it in a pilaf. Serve this with the Piri Piri Grilled Shrimp appetizer on page 37 to make a healthful meal.

1 cup black-eyed peas, soaked overnight
4 cups water
1½ teaspoons coarse salt
½ pound snow peas, trimmed
1 tablespoon unsalted butter
1 tablespoon vegetable or olive oil
1 onion, minced
2 cloves garlic, minced
1½ cups uncooked basmati rice
3 cups vegetable stock
¼ teaspoon freshly ground white pepper
½ pound fresh, shelled English peas or
   frozen green peas
2 tablespoons chopped parsley
1 tablespoon lemon zest
Fresh pea shoots, for garnish (optional)

In a small pot, cover black-eyed peas with water. Bring to a boil, skimming off any impurities, and cook 20 minutes, or until soft but not mushy. Bring the water to a boil, add 1 teaspoon salt, and cook snow peas 1 minute, or until they turn a vibrant green but are still crunchy. Drain snow peas, and cover with cold water; strain and set aside. Cut the snow peas into julienned strips.

In a large skillet over medium heat, add butter and oil; cook onion and garlic until soft, about 5 minutes. Add rice and cook an additional 5 minutes. Add stock, remaining ½ teaspoon salt, and white pepper; bring to a boil, and then reduce to a simmer. Continue to cook, covered, ½ hour. Add reserved snow peas, English peas, black-eyed peas, parsley, and zest. Mix well and adjust seasonings to taste. Garnish with pea shoots if desired.

yam rösti

Makes 4 rösti

This Swiss "potato cake," usually made with russet potatoes, is similar to hash browns. Yams work better than sweet potatoes here because their higher starch content helps the rösti hold together. This is an elegant side dish, especially suited to accompany the Lamb Chops with Brandied Peach Chutney on page 66.

1½ pounds yams, washed and scrubbed clean
4 tablespoons all-purpose flour
½ teaspoon coarse salt
¼ teaspoon freshly ground white pepper
2 tablespoons unsalted butter

Preheat the oven to 350°F. Wrap yams individually in foil and bake 1 hour, or until a small paring knife easily penetrates the flesh. Remove yams from foil, and refrigerate until completely cooled. Peel cooled yams with a vegetable peeler or sharp paring knife. Using a box grater, grate yams; toss in a bowl with flour, and salt and white pepper.

Heat a small nonstick skillet over medium-high heat. Add ½ tablespoon butter and a quarter of the shredded yams. Press yams into skillet, and cook for 3 minutes, and then turn and cook 3 minutes. Repeat with remaining shredded yams. Keep warm in a low oven until ready to serve.

haricots verts and vidalia onion sauté

Makes 4 servings

Haricots verts are a variety of French green beans that are extra thin and have a more delicate flavor than their common green-bean cousin. The Vidalia onion has a juicy sweetness that complements the haricots verts. This dish is a wonderful addition to the Hickory and Maple-Glazed Pork Tenderloin on page 69.

1 teaspoon coarse salt, plus more to taste
1 pound haricots verts (French green beans)
1½ tablespoons olive oil
1 Vidalia onion, sliced thin
Freshly ground black pepper

Bring a large pot of water to a boil and add 1 teaspoon salt. Add haricots verts and cook 4 to 5 minutes, or until the beans are bright green and bend slightly. Drain and cover in cold water to stop the cooking process. Drain again and lay on paper towels to dry.

In a large skillet, heat olive oil over medium-high heat. Add onion slices and prepared haricots verts. Season with salt and pepper to taste. Cook until onions are soft and haricot verts are heated through, about 6 to 7 minutes.

okra tempura

Makes 4 servings

This preparation of okra may convert the surest skeptics. The quick and light cooking method keeps the okra from developing its signature mucilaginous quality. As a simple side dish, this tempura is a nice change from other green vegetables. Try it dipped in the West African Peanut Sauce on page 149.

1 pound fresh okra
1 large egg
1 cup ice water
1¼ cups all-purpose flour
4 cups vegetable or peanut oil
Coarse salt
Freshly ground white pepper

Cut off hard tops of okra and slice lengthwise. In a medium bowl, whisk together egg and the ice water. Stir in flour until mixture just comes together (do not overmix).

In a medium heavy pot, heat oil to 370°F. Toss okra in flour mixture until lightly coated. Add enough okra to the pot as not to overcrowd, and cook 4 to 5 minutes, until light brown. Adjust heat to maintain temperature, if necessary. When finished cooking, drain okra on paper towels and season with salt and white pepper to taste. Serve immediately.

sweet potato salad

Makes 6 servings

This recipe is a refreshing alternative to the classic potato salad. I love the versatility of this sweet vegetable: you can substitute it in just about any savory recipe that uses regular potatoes, and you can bake or boil it and use the puree in desserts. This is the perfect match for the Molasses-Barbecued Chicken on page 57.

2 pounds sweet potatoes, peeled and diced
½ teaspoon coarse salt, plus more to taste
1 bunch green onions, chopped
1 rib celery, finely chopped
2 tablespoons chopped parsley
½ cup mayonnaise or sour cream
1 teaspoon celery seed
½ teaspoon paprika
⅛ teaspoon cayenne pepper
¼ teaspoon freshly ground white pepper

Place prepared sweet potatoes in a small pot and cover with water; add the salt and cook 8 to 10 minutes, or until fork-tender. Drain, and toss with the remaining ingredients while warm.

fig, pecan, and sausage cornbread stuffing

Makes 8 servings

The combination of figs, pecans, sausage, and cornbread is absolute perfection in its gathering of these well-loved Southern ingredients. This dish has so much flavor that its best with a simply prepared recipe, such as the Buttermilk and Sage-Soaked Turkey Breast on page 64. When you prepare the Confetti Cornbread for this stuffing, omit the chiles, bell pepper, and green onions.

1 pound pork sausage (preferably spicy Italian)

1 cup Madeira wine

¾ pound dried Calmyrna figs, stemmed and cut into eighths (about 2 cups)

2 cups pecan pieces

1 cup (2 sticks) unsalted butter

3 cups finely chopped onions

1½ cups finely chopped celery

2 tablespoons chopped sage

2 tablespoons chopped thyme

2 tablespoons chopped rosemary

2½ teaspoons coarse salt

1 teaspoon freshly ground white pepper

1 recipe plain Confetti Cornbread (see recipe, page 125), cooled and crumbled

Preheat the oven to 350°F. Remove sausage from casing, if necessary, and crumble. In a medium skillet over medium heat, cook sausage until cooked through; set aside. In a small saucepan over medium heat, add Madeira and figs. Cook 10 minutes, or until all liquid is evaporated.

Preheat the oven to 350°F. In a small skillet over low heat, toast pecans 5 minutes, or until light brown and slightly fragrant. In a large skillet over medium heat, melt butter; add onions and celery, and cook until vegetables are soft and translucent, about 10 minutes. Add sage, thyme, rosemary, salt, and white pepper, and cook an additional 5 minutes. In a large bowl mix the reserved sausage, figs, and onion mixture with the crumbled cornbread, and loosely mix with a wooden spoon. Gently press stuffing mixture into a glass or ceramic 12 x 8¼ x 2½-inch baking dish; the top should be textured and rustic, not smooth. Bake 1 hour. Serve immediately.

sweet corn pudding soufflé

Makes 6 to 8 servings

This dish is easy to make and less rich than it may appear. There are many varieties of corn, but juicy, sweet corn found in the middle of the summer is the best. Corn is a grain that is native to the Americas, and so naturally it has been used into soul food cooking for several generations. This soufflé is a lovely foil for the flavorful North African Spiced Salmon on page 50.

3 to 4 ears corn, shucked
1½ tablespoons unsalted butter
2 tablespoons all-purpose flour
1 cup milk, heated
4 large egg yolks
2 tablespoons half-and-half
1 teaspoon coarse salt
½ teaspoon freshly ground white pepper
1 teaspoon sugar
¼ teaspoon freshly grated nutmeg
6 large egg whites
1 tablespoon softened butter, for greasing
Flour, for dusting

Preheat the oven to 350°F. Place shucked ears of corn in a pot of boiling water. Cook 7 to 8 minutes, just until corn is tender. Remove corn and let cool; using a sharp knife, cut kernels from the cobs.

In a small saucepan over medium heat, melt butter, and then slowly whisk in flour. Cook 2 minutes, and then slowly add milk. Cook about 5 minutes, stirring constantly, until sauce thickens. Slowly whisk in egg yolks. Cook 3 minutes, stirring constantly, and then add half-and-half, salt, white pepper, sugar, and nutmeg. Fold prepared corn into sauce. Scrape into clean mixing bowl, and set aside.

Grease and flour a 10-inch soufflé dish. In a clean, dry bowl, beat egg whites until soft peaks form. Add half of egg whites to corn mixture. Continue whisking remaining egg whites until stiff. Fold into corn mixture. Pour mixture into prepared soufflé dish, and bake 20 to 25 minutes, until top is lightly brown and filling is set.

yucca gratin

Makes 6 to 8 servings

I love the starchy texture and natural sweetness of the root vegetable yucca, or cassava, and it doesn't need much to embellish its flavor. I was introduced to it nearly seven years ago while working in a Caribbean-influenced restaurant, and it's also a major staple in the diet of today's African people. It's a perfect match for the Jamaican Curried Oxtail on page 71.

2½ pounds yucca
Coarse salt
Freshly ground white pepper
Freshly grated nutmeg
½ pint heavy cream

Preheat the oven to 350°F. Use a sharp vegetable peeler to carefully remove the brown waxy skin from yucca, making sure no red-tinted flesh remains. Slice yucca into ⅛-inch rounds and place a layer on the bottom of a 1½-quart baking dish. Sprinkle lightly with salt, white pepper, and nutmeg to taste. Cover with cream and repeat process until all the yucca is used. Bake 1 hour, or until the top is brown and a knife inserted into the center comes out clean, basting with the hot cream in the bottom of the dish every 10 minutes.

steamed collard greens
with red onions and smoked turkey

Makes 6 servings

Collard greens are synonymous with soul food cooking in the way that pasta is with Italian cooking. This robust green is the heavyweight of the cabbage family. I've replaced the traditional ham hock with smoked turkey drumstick to lighten up the dish. This is also a quick-cooking method that helps to retain this excellent source of vitamin C, and it has a low fat content. This is a delicious match for the Molasses-Barbecued Chicken on page 57.

1 smoked turkey drumstick
2 cups chicken stock
4 cloves garlic, minced
1 teaspoon crushed red pepper
4 pounds collard greens, cleaned and
**   large stems removed**
1 red onion, sliced into rings
¼ cup cider vinegar
Coarse salt
Freshly ground black pepper

In a large pot over medium heat, add turkey, stock, garlic, and crushed red pepper. Simmer, covered, until turkey heats through and meat can be easily picked from the bone, about 30 minutes. Remove drumstick from pot and remove meat. Return meat to pot, and discard bone.

Meanwhile, prepare collard greens by stacking the leaves and rolling them like a cigar, and then slicing into thin strips. Add greens and onion to pot with turkey. As greens wilt, slowly add cider vinegar. Season with salt and pepper to taste.

sweet and sour mustard greens

Makes 4 servings

Like most greens, mustard greens are an excellent source of vitamins A and C, iron, and potassium. They can be eaten raw or cooked, but I like to lessen their spicy bite with a bit of a sugar-and-vinegar reduction called gastrique sauce. This dish is a great addition to the Pan-Roasted Halibut with Roasted Beet Tapenade on page 52. Any leftover gastrique sauce will keep refrigerated in an airtight container up to one month.

½ **cup cider vinegar**
½ **cup sugar**
2 tablespoons vegetable oil
¼ **cup chopped shallots**
**2 pounds mustard greens, washed and
  chopped into 2-inch pieces**
Coarse salt
Freshly ground black pepper

In a small saucepan over medium heat, cook vinegar and sugar until a thick syrup forms, about 20 minutes. In a large skillet over medium heat, add vegetable oil, shallots, and greens. Cook 5 minutes, sprinkling with water until greens are wilted. Season with salt and pepper to taste, and add 2 tablespoons of the vinegar-sugar mixture. Serve immediately.

spinach spoonbread

Makes 8 servings

Spoonbread is a Southern specialty that's a cross between cornbread and a souf-flé. It was probably created because of the need not to waste anything, including buttermilk—literally the milk that remained after butter was churned. I've incorporated spinach into this recipe to liven it up. Its familiar taste and texture make it an appropriate accompaniment for almost any main dish in the second chapter. The spoonbread can also be made in individual ramekins; the cooking time will be reduced, so test by inserting a toothpick in the center—it should come out clean.

1 teaspoon coarse salt, plus more to taste
½ pound fresh spinach leaves,
washed and drained
1 cup cornmeal
3 cups buttermilk
3 large eggs, separated
1½ teaspoons baking soda
¼ teaspoon freshly ground white pepper,
plus more to taste
3 tablespoons unsalted butter, melted
⅛ teaspoon nutmeg
1 head garlic, roasted (instructions follow)
Vegetable spray

Preheat oven to 350°F. Bring a small pot of water to a boil, and add ½ teaspoon salt and the spinach. When spinach wilts, drain in a colander and run cold water over spinach until it is completely cool.

Whisk together cornmeal, buttermilk, egg yolks, the remaining ½ teaspoon salt, baking soda, white pepper, butter, nutmeg, and roasted garlic. In a clean, dry bowl, using an electric hand mixer, beat egg whites until stiff peaks form. Fold egg whites into cornmeal mixture. Spray a 2-quart baking dish with vegetable spray and add spoonbread batter. Bake spoonbread 30 minutes, or until lightly browned on top and a toothpick inserted in the center comes out clean.

ROASTED GARLIC Preheat oven to 300°F. Cut the top off the head of garlic, and place both pieces on foil. Mix 1 teaspoon water and ½ teaspoon olive oil, and drizzle over garlic. Sprinkle with coarse salt and freshly ground black pepper. Close foil and roast 1 hour, or until garlic cloves ooze from their papery skins. Squeeze out the roasted garlic and use as needed.

green cabbage and green onion slaw

Makes 8 servings

A proper Southern barbecue is all about side dishes, and slaw is one of the most popular. Often it is mayonnaise based or vinegar based, but this recipe is the perfect blend of both. And even if you're not serving barbecue, it makes a great side dish on most any table: the cabbage keeps its fresh crunch and always provides a pleasant contrast to a dish with tender meat or vegetables. Try it with the Mustard Barbecued Cornish Game Hens on page 63.

¾ cup minced red onion
1 jalapeño chile, chopped
2 cloves garlic, minced
2 tablespoons fresh chopped parsley
1 tablespoon Dijon-style mustard
1 tablespoon sour cream
1 tablespoon sugar
¾ cup canola oil
1 teaspoon coarse salt
¼ teaspoon freshly ground white pepper
3 tablespoons brown mustard seeds
1 head of green cabbage, sliced thin
1½ bunches of green onions, julienned

In a food processor, place onion, jalapeño, garlic, parsley, mustard, sour cream, sugar, canola oil, salt, white pepper, and mustard seeds; process 1 minute, or until fully blended. Transfer the mixture to a medium bowl, and toss with cabbage and green onions. Refrigerate until ready to serve.

chopped dandelion greens

with red pepper, hazelnuts, garlic chips, and warm sherry vinegar dressing

Makes 4 servings

Cultivated dandelion greens are a great addition to the greens repertoire. They can be eaten raw or cooked, but I prefer them a little in between. The combination of a slightly sweet dressing, roasted peppers, and toasted nuts rounds out the pleasant bitterness of the greens. Pair this with the Brown Sugar and Pineapple-glazed Ribs on page 41 for a complete meal.

1 head garlic, peeled
⅔ cup milk
⅔ cup vegetable oil
2 tablespoons sherry vinegar
1 tablespoon extra-virgin olive oil
1 teaspoon Dijon-style mustard
1 teaspoon honey
2 pounds dandelion greens, washed and
   chopped into 2-inch pieces
1 red bell pepper, cored, seeded, and julienned
Coarse salt
Freshly ground black pepper
½ cup chopped hazelnuts, toasted

Slice garlic cloves as thinly as possible. Place garlic in a small saucepan and add ⅓ cup milk. Bring to a boil and strain. (Discard liquid or use to make mashed potatoes or macaroni and cheese.)

Repeat this process with remaining milk. This helps keep the garlic chips from tasting bitter when browning. Place garlic slices on a paper towel; set aside.

In a large skillet, heat vegetable oil over medium-high heat. Add a third of the garlic slices, and cook just until they begin to darken. Using a slotted spoon, transfer the garlic chips to a clean paper towel. Repeat with remaining garlic chips, cooking in three batches.

Pour off oil from skillet. Return skillet to burner and reduce heat to medium; add vinegar, oil, mustard, and honey, and stir to combine. Slowly stir in dandelion greens and bell pepper, continuing to add more as they soften, about 5 minutes. Season with salt and pepper to taste. Add garlic chips and toasted hazelnuts; stir to combine.

yukon gold potato hash
with bacon and bell peppers

Makes 6 servings

This is another great recipe that I owe to my father. It's an ode to our weekend brunches when I was a child, which often included a potato hash when he usually cleaned out the refrigerator of leftover onions and peppers. My dad claims that he grew up eating potatoes at every meal, so he had to be innovative. Here I've added delicious Yukon gold potatoes to update my childhood favorite. Pair it with the Poached Salmon-and-Potato Cakes on page 33 to make a great brunch.

8 Yukon gold potatoes, diced
6 slices of thick-cut bacon, cut into 1-inch
**   pieces**
1 onion, diced
2 cloves garlic, minced
1 green bell pepper, cored, seeded,
**   and diced**
1 red bell pepper, cored, seeded,
**   and diced**
Coarse salt
Freshly ground white pepper
Fresh chopped parsley, for garnish

Place potatoes in a 2-quart saucepan, and cover with water. Bring to a boil, and cook until fork-tender. Drain and set aside to cool.

In a large cast-iron skillet, cook bacon to render fat. Strain fat from bacon; set aside. Place bacon on paper towels; set aside. Use 2 tablespoons of bacon drippings to cook onion, garlic, and bell peppers until soft, 5 to 7 minutes. Add potatoes, and cook until tender and crispy. Add reserved bacon and season with salt and white pepper to taste. Garnish with parsley.

fingerling potato salad

Makes 6 servings

Almost every picnic or buffet that I've attended features someone's secret potato salad recipe. Everyone has his or her favorite additions, such as cooked eggs, pickled relishes, olives—the list goes on and on. I prefer to serve a simply dressed salad and feature a special potato. It's also a healthier version than most. The spicy Blackened Tilapia on page 54 is a great match for this flavorful side.

2 pounds fingerling or other heirloom potatoes
1 teaspoon coarse salt, plus more to taste
1 tablespoon roasted garlic
   (see instructions, page 98)
2½ teaspoons Dijon-style mustard
½ cup red-wine vinegar
1½ cups olive oil
Freshly ground white pepper
1 medium red onion, cut in half and sliced thin
1 tablespoon yellow mustard seeds
⅓ cup chopped herbs (parsley, tarragon, thyme, chervil)
2 bunches watercress, washed and stems removed

Wash and slice potatoes into bite-size pieces. Place potatoes in a small pot, cover with water, and add 1 teaspoon salt. Cook potatoes over medium-high heat until fork-tender.

To make vinaigrette, whisk garlic, mustard, and vinegar in a bowl, then slowly whisk in olive oil, and season with salt and white pepper to taste. Drain cooked potatoes, and toss in vinaigrette while potatoes are warm. Add onion, mustard seeds, and herbs. Toss with watercress just before serving.

baked goods,
DESSERTS,
sweets,
BISCUITS

Anyone who has spent time in a household where soul food and Southern food are served knows about the dessert specialties. That's where I developed my sweet tooth. Sugar was one of the most important crops in Colonial times, and it was used extensively in both sweet and savory recipes. This was long before people realized the health ramifications of a diet too high in simple carbohydrates. So remember: everything in moderation.

watermelon sorbet
with brown sugar tuiles

Makes 1 quart sorbet

Refreshing and light, this watermelon sorbet makes a pleasant end to a spicy flavorful meal. The tuiles are a simple wafer cookie and are easy to make with a little practice. The sorbet by itself makes a nice palate cleanser.

1 cup water
1½ cups sugar
3½ cups seedless watermelon flesh, about
   3½ pound wedge
2 lemons, juiced (about 3 tablespoons)
Pinch coarse salt
Brown Sugar Tuiles (recipe follows)

Heat the water and sugar in a small saucepan over medium-high heat until sugar is dissolved. Remove and let cool, and then transfer to the refrigerator to chill. Place watermelon in a food processor, and puree. In a large bowl mix pureed watermelon with chilled sugar syrup, lemon juice, and salt. Freeze mixture in an ice cream maker, according to the manufacturer's instructions.

BROWN SUGAR TUILES
Makes 36 tuiles

The tuiles can be shaped immediately after they are removed from the oven. If you desire, roll them like a cigar, a cone, or a bowl, which is great for serving the sorbet. Also, you can make curved tuiles by resting them over the handle of a wooden spoon. They taste the same, flat or shaped.

4 large egg whites
1¼ cups all-purpose flour
1 cup light-brown sugar, firmly packed
6 tablespoons unsalted butter, melted
   and cooled
2 tablespoons heavy cream

Preheat the oven to 450°F. In a medium bowl, whisk together ingredients. Using a Silpat (see note, page 108), spread 2 teaspoons into thin 3½-inch circles. Make sure to spread the batter thinly and evenly: If circles are too thick, the tuiles will be chewy rather than crisp. Bake 3 to 4 minutes, or until slightly firm.

banana pudding napoleon

Makes 18 tuiles or 6 napoleons

I was practically weaned on vanilla wafer banana pudding. Using homemade cookies makes all the difference in my version, but the original flavor remains to create a bit of nostalgia. The silicone French baking mat, known as a Silpat, found in most kitchen-supply stores is an invaluable tool in making these tuiles.

3 large egg whites
½ cup plus 1 tablespoon sugar
6 tablespoons unsalted butter, melted
½ teaspoon pure vanilla extract
½ cup plus 1 tablespoon all-purpose flour
2 firm, ripe bananas
Banana Pudding (recipe follows)
Confectioners' sugar, for dusting

Preheat the oven to 350°F. Whisk egg whites with sugar. Stir in melted butter and vanilla extract. Fold in flour. Line a baking pan with a Silpat, and spread 1 tablespoon of mixture thin in a circle of about 4 inches in diameter. Repeat to form 18 tuiles. Bake until light brown, about 5 minutes. Bake in two batches if necessary.

For each serving, use 3 tuiles. Slice bananas on a diagonal. On each plate, place 1 cookie, followed by 2 slices of bananas, then ¼ cup banana pudding. Repeat, and then top with remaining cookie. Dust with confectioners' sugar.

BANANA PUDDING
Makes 3 cups

2½ cups whole milk
⅓ cup plus 3 tablespoons sugar
2 large eggs
1 large egg yolk
¼ cup cornstarch
2 teaspoons pure vanilla extract
1 tablespoon unsalted butter, melted
2 firm, ripe bananas

In a small bowl, whisk together ½ cup milk, ⅓ cup sugar, eggs, egg yolk, and cornstarch. In a medium saucepan, bring 2 cups milk and 3 tablespoons sugar to a low boil. Whisk constantly until thickened and smooth, about 2 minutes. Remove pan from heat. Strain custard, and whisk in vanilla and butter. Dice the bananas into small pieces. Fold banana pieces into custard, and refrigerate until set.

chocolate pound cake
with orange-pomegranate custard sauce

Makes 6 to 8 servings

Pound cake reminds me of church bake sales that take place regularly in the South to raise money for various clubs and committees. Certain members were known for their secret recipes. They all varied slightly, even though the basic ingredients are sugar, butter, flour, and eggs. The addition of chocolate adds a richness that speaks for itself.

½ cup (1 stick) unsalted butter, softened
1⅔ cups sugar
5 large eggs
2 cups sifted unbleached flour
½ cup good quality dark cocoa powder
½ teaspoon coarse salt
8 ounces dark chocolate
1 teaspoon pure vanilla extract
½ cup sour cream
Orange-Pomegranate Custard Sauce
   (recipe follows)

Preheat the oven to 325°F. Butter and flour the bottom of a 9½ x 5½ x 2¾-inch loaf pan, and set aside.

In a large bowl, cream together butter and sugar. Add eggs, one at a time. In a separate bowl, sift together flour, cocoa powder, and salt. Melt chocolate in a small bowl set over a pot of simmering water, and set aside to cool.

Combine flour mixture and butter mixture; fold in vanilla, sour cream, and chocolate. Pour mixture into loaf pan and bake 1½ hours, or until a toothpick inserted into the center comes out clean. (After 1 hour, check the cake every 10 minutes, since oven temperatures vary.) Remove pan, and place on a rack to cool 5 minutes before unmolding. Serve with Orange-Pomegranate Custard Sauce.

ORANGE-POMEGRANATE CUSTARD SAUCE
Makes 6 to 8 servings

2 cups milk
Zest of 2 oranges
1 teaspoon pure vanilla extract
6 large egg yolks
⅓ cup sugar
Pinch coarse salt
2 tablespoons Cointreau or other orange
   liqueur (optional)
Seeds of 1 pomegranate

In a medium saucepan over high heat, scald milk with zest and vanilla. Turn off heat and let mixture rest 10 minutes. In a medium bowl, whisk together egg yolks, sugar, and salt. Slowly whisk milk mixture into egg yolks, and then return to saucepan. Cook custard over low heat about 5 minutes, stirring constantly with a wooden spoon. Once custard has thickened enough to coat the spoon, remove from heat and strain. Stir in Cointreau, if using. Cover and transfer to the refrigerator to chill, 2 hours, or up to 2 days. Add pomegranate seeds just before serving.

chocolate bourbon cherry pecan squares

Makes 36 squares

Rich chocolate, sweet bourbon-soaked cherries, and crunchy pecans all in one bite! My aunt Maxine has been making these for years, and she has been kind enough to allow me to share this recipe with you. The squares keep well in an airtight container in the refrigerator for up to two weeks.

2 cups packed dark-brown sugar
1 cup heavy cream
10 ounces dark chocolate
⅔ cup dried pitted cherries, cut in half
½ cup bourbon
⅔ cup pecan pieces, toasted
¼ cup dark cocoa powder

In a small nonreactive saucepan over high heat, bring sugar and heavy cream to a boil. (Watch closely that the mixture does not overflow.) Reduce heat to medium-high. Continue to cook mixture until it reaches 238°F on a candy thermometer, about 15 minutes. Meanwhile, chop chocolate and place in a small stainless steel bowl over a pot of simmering water to melt. When chocolate has melted, set aside.

Once sugar mixture reaches desired temperature, remove from heat and allow to cool to 160°F. Place cherries and bourbon in a small saucepan over medium heat, and cook until most of the bourbon has evaporated and the cherries are plump. Fold chocolate, pecans, and bourbon-soaked cherries into sugar mixture. Pour mixture into 8-inch-square baking dish, and transfer to the refrigerator to harden, about 2 hours. Cut into 1½-inch squares and roll in cocoa powder.

raspberry grit parfaits

Makes 6 servings

At the Greenbrier, a resort in White Sulphur Springs, West Virginia, I discovered this amazing dessert. It was a flavor and texture combination that I had never tasted before: the tangy sweetness of raspberries coupled with the gritty consistency of, well, grits. This is an easy dessert to make and looks vivid and impressive when served. Children love this treat and can lend a hand in making it.

3 cups water
1 cup instant grits
½ teaspoon coarse salt, plus dash
1½ pounds quick-frozen raspberries, thawed
½ cup plus 1 tablespoon granulated sugar
¼ cup crème de framboise (raspberry liqueur)
2 teaspoons lemon zest
½ pint whipping cream
Mint sprigs, for garnish (optional)

Bring the water to a boil in a small saucepan, and then add grits and ½ teaspoon salt. Cook 5 minutes, stirring continuously, until thick but not dry. Allow grits to cool. In a medium bowl, combine raspberries, ½ cup sugar, liqueur, 1 teaspoon zest, and a dash of salt, and let stand 2 hours or overnight. Place raspberry mixture in a food processor, and pulse 3 to 4 times. Stir in cooled grits. In a large bowl, whip cream with 1 tablespoon sugar. When cream is almost stiff, add remaining lemon zest and continue to whip until stiff. Spoon alternate layers of raspberry grits and lemon whipped cream into 6 parfait glasses. Top with a sprig of mint if desired.

gingerbread crêpes
with caramelized apples and rum hard sauce

Makes 6 servings

The smell of ginger baking is a luringly seductive scent. The West Indian culture has the Chinese and East Indian explorers to thank for bringing this wonderfully pungent ingredient to the islands. It's used in many forms in both sweet and savory dishes, but one of my favorites is ginger beer, a fiery nonalcoholic drink. These crêpes are great when you don't have time to bake a cake but still want to make something impressive and immensely satisfying.

1½ cups milk
3 large eggs
¼ cup sugar
4 tablespoons molasses
1½ teaspoons grated ginger
1½ cups all-purpose flour
1 tablespoon baking powder
½ teaspoon ground ginger
¼ teaspoon ground cinnamon
⅛ teaspoon freshly ground white pepper
Pinch ground cloves
Pinch coarse salt
3 tablespoons unsalted butter, melted
Vegetable spray
Carmelized Apples (recipe follows)
1 pint vanilla ice cream
Rum Hard Sauce (recipe follows)

In a medium bowl, whisk together milk, eggs, sugar, molasses, and grated ginger. In a small bowl, sift together flour, baking powder, ground ginger, cinnamon, white pepper, cloves, and salt. Slowly whisk flour mixture into milk mixture. Add melted butter. Let batter sit 1 hour.

Heat an 8-inch crêpe pan or nonstick skillet over medium-high heat. Spray pan generously with vegetable spray, and add 3 tablespoons crêpe batter. Swirl to completely coat bottom of pan with a thin layer. Cook about 1 minute, until almost dry on the top and lightly browned on the edges. Using a thin spatula, turn and cook other side about 15 seconds, or until lightly browned. Place crêpes on a plate with a piece of waxed paper between each crêpe. (The crêpes can be covered with plastic wrap until ready for serving. Reheat in 200°F oven 5 minutes.)

To serve, place a crêpe in the center of each plate and fill with ⅓ cup Carmelized Apples. Top with 1 scoop vanilla ice cream and 2 tablespoons Rum Hard Sauce.

CARMELIZED APPLES

Makes about 2 cups

Tart Granny Smith apples work well in this recipe. It can be made a day in advance, covered with plastic wrap and stored in the refrigerator. Reheat over medium heat before serving.

2 tablespoons unsalted butter
4 tart apples, peeled, cored and sliced thin
⅓ cup sugar

In a medium skillet, add butter, apples, and sugar. Cook until apples are soft and caramelized.

RUM HARD SAUCE

Makes about 1 cup

1 large egg
½ cup sugar
½ cup (1 stick) unsalted butter, melted
¼ cup dark rum

Whisk together egg and sugar in a small bowl set over a pot of simmering water. Continue to whisk mixture until light and creamy, 5 minutes. Slowly whisk in melted butter, and then rum.

sweet potato cheesecake with candied pecans

Makes 8 to 10 servings

Sweet potatoes are a recurring theme throughout this book—not only because they're my favorite, but also because they're so important in soul food cuisine. They're an excellent source of vitamin A and naturally low in fat. You can make the puree from the baked sweet potato one day in advance.

1½ pounds cream cheese, softened
1¼ cups granulated sugar
Pinch coarse salt
5 large eggs
2 large egg yolks
½ cup sour cream
1 teaspoon pure vanilla extract
¼ teaspoon ground ginger
¼ teaspoon ground cinnamon
⅛ teaspoon freshly grated nutmeg
3 tablespoons all-purpose flour
2 cups Sweet Potato Puree (recipe follows)
Graham Cracker Crust (recipe follows)
Candied Pecans (recipe follows)

Preheat the oven to 325°F. Place cream cheese in the bowl of an electric mixer fitted with the paddle attachment. Beat until smooth. Continue to mix, adding sugar and salt. Add the eggs and yolks one at a time, and then add sour cream, vanilla, and spices. Reduce speed to low, and then slowly add flour and Sweet Potato Puree. Pour the batter into crust-lined pan. Place in the oven on the center rack.

Place a baking pan of hot water under cheesecake. Bake 70 minutes. To test for doneness, insert a skewer or sharp paring knife; the batter should adhere and be crumbly. Remove cheesecake from oven, and place pan on rack to cool 30 minutes. Wrap in plastic while still in pan, and transfer to refrigerate to cool completely. Loosen plastic, and remove cheesecake. Carefully slice cake with a knife dipped in hot water and then wiped dry. Reserve ¼ cup of the candied pecans, and finely chop the remainder. Sprinkle over the top of the cake, and place the reserved whole pecans around the perimeter of the cake.

SWEET POTATO PUREE
Makes 2 cups

2 large or 3 medium sweet potatoes

Preheat the oven to 350°F. Prick unpeeled sweet potatoes with a fork, and then wrap in foil and bake 45 minutes to 1 hour—a knife should easily penetrate the flesh of the potatoes when fully cooked. Cool completely, and peel. Place potatoes in a food processor, and pulse to puree.

GRAHAM CRACKER CRUST
Makes 1 nine-inch crust

**1½ cups graham cracker crumbs
(about 12 rectangular crackers)
¼ cup sifted confectioners' sugar
4 tablespoons unsalted butter, melted**

Preheat oven to 375°F. Place graham crackers in food processor, and process until fine. Measure 1½ cups, and combine with confectioners' sugar and butter. Press mixture into a 9-inch springform pan, and transfer to the refrigerator to chill 30 minutes, or overnight. Bake crust 10 minutes. Transfer to rack to cool.

CANDIED PECANS
Makes 1 cup

**1 cup granulated sugar
1 cup pecan halves, toasted
Softened unsalted butter, for greasing**

In a small nonreactive saucepan over medium-high heat, melt 1 cup granulated sugar and cook until it turns dark amber. Stir in nuts until completely coated. Pour onto buttered baking sheet or Silpat (see note, page 108). Keep nuts in individual pieces. Let cool before using.

mango tart tatin
with spice island ice cream

Makes 4 servings

The traditional tart Tatin is an upside down tart made with apples, but this version is made with mango, another contribution made by the East Indian explorers to the Caribbean islands. It's common to find the unripe green mangoes in savory dishes there, but when ripe, this fruit has a distinctive perfumed sweetness. A deliciously spicy ice cream recipe accompanies the tart. Use 4½- to 5-inch cast-iron blini pans for individual servings.

2 cups all-purpose flour
7 tablespoons unsalted butter, diced and
  chilled
1 large egg yolk
3 tablespoons confectioners' sugar
½ teaspoon coarse salt
1 cup granulated sugar
½ cup water
3 large slightly ripened mangoes, sliced thin
Spice Island Ice Cream (recipe follows)

Make pastry dough by placing flour, 5 tablespoons butter, egg yolk, confectioners' sugar, and salt in food processor and pulsing until texture resembles a coarse meal; add 4 to 6 tablespoons of ice water, one tablespoon at a time, as necessary. Lightly form dough into small ball, wrap in plastic wrap, and press to flatten into a disk. Transfer to refrigerator to chill 30 minutes.

Remove dough and roll out ⅛-inch thick, and with a sharp paring knife, cut into 4¼-inch rounds using a 5-inch saucer as template. Using a spatula, stack on a plate with waxed paper between each round. Transfer rounds to refrigerator to chill 30 minutes.

Preheat the oven to 400°F, and heat individual pans. Make caramel by placing granulated sugar and the water in a small nonreactive pan over medium-high heat, stirring constantly. When sugar mixture is amber, place pot in bowl of ice water to stop the cooking process. Pour caramel mixture into hot pans, and fill with mango slices. Melt the remaining 2 tablespoons butter, and brush on mango slices. Prick pastry rounds and place on top of mango. Bake tarts 25 minutes, or until pastry is lightly browned. Serve with Spice Island Ice Cream.

SPICE ISLAND ICE CREAM

Makes 1 pint

2 cups milk
1 vanilla bean
2 cinnamon sticks
3 cloves
¼ teaspoon freshly ground white pepper
¼ teaspoon ground ginger
Pinch ground allspice
Pinch coarse salt
6 large egg yolks
⅔ cups sugar
½ cup heavy cream, lightly whipped
2 tablespoons molasses

In a small saucepan scald milk with vanilla bean, spices, and salt, and set aside 10 minutes so flavors infuse. In a large bowl whisk egg yolks with sugar until the mixture is light and fluffy, about 5 minutes. Slowly whisk hot milk mixture into egg mixture. Strain combined mixtures into a large bowl and cool by placing inside another bowl filled with ice water. Fold in whipped heavy cream. Freeze in an ice cream maker according to manufacturer's instructions. About a quarter of the time into the freezing process, drizzle in molasses.

lemon chess tartlettes

Makes 10 servings

A bright citrus taste at the end of a rich meal enlivens the palate. Chess pie, a Southern favorite, can feature buttermilk or even chocolate flavors, but I enjoy the lemon versions the best. This one is intensely sweet and simple. The individual servings are perfect for the finale of an elegant dinner.

8 tablespoons (1 stick) unsalted butter
2 cups sugar
7 large egg yolks
Zest of 4 lemons, about 2 tablespoons
1½ teaspoons pure vanilla extract
½ cup heavy cream
3 tablespoons cornmeal
Tart Crust (recipe follows)

Preheat the oven to 350°F. Cream together the butter and sugar. Add yolks, zest, vanilla, and cream. Fold in cornmeal. Pour into unbaked Tart Crust, and bake 35 to 40 minutes, until set. The filling should be firm, but not too crisp.

TART CRUST
Makes 10 four-inch tarts

2¼ cups all-purpose flour
1 cup (2 sticks) unsalted butter, diced
   and chilled
1 teaspoon coarse salt

Place the flour, butter, and salt into the bowl of a food processor. Pulse mixture until butter resembles small peas. Slowly add 5 to 7 tablespoons of ice water until the dough forms into a ball.

Turn out dough onto a lightly floured surface. Using the palm of your hand, flatten dough against the surface forming one piece; butter pieces should be visible. Press into plastic wrap and shape into a disk. Chill at least ½ hour, up to 24 hours. Divide dough into 10 equal pieces. Roll out each piece to a ⅛-inch thickness to line tart pans. Transfer to the refrigerator to chill an additional 30 minutes.

benne crescent wafers

with spiced georgia peach sorbet

Makes 3 dozen cookies

West Africans, who worked in the rice fields of Georgia and the Carolinas, brought crunchy sesame seeds to this continent. This unusual ingredient has taken on a life of its own as the local confectionery favorite in the Southwest.

¾ cup raw sesame seeds
¾ cup (1½ sticks) unsalted butter, softened
¼ cup granulated sugar
¼ cup light-brown sugar
1 teaspoon pure vanilla extract
2 tablespoons pure maple syrup
¼ teaspoon coarse salt
2 cups all-purpose flour
Confectioners' sugar, for rolling
Peach Sorbet (recipe follows)

Preheat the oven to 300°F. Spread seeds on a baking sheet. Toast seeds 15 minutes, or until evenly golden brown. Combine the butter and sugars in a mixing bowl, and beat until creamy. Blend in vanilla, maple syrup, and salt. Stir in flour and toasted sesame seeds, and mix well. Place dough on a lightly floured surface and roll into ½-inch-thick cylinder; wrap in plastic wrap and chill 1 hour or up to 24 hours.

On a lightly floured surface, cut chilled dough into 1½-inch strips. Form crescents by rolling strips the thickness of your index finger. Place on a non-stick baking sheet. Transfer to refrigerator to chill 30 minutes. Remove, and bake 35 minutes, or until light brown. Cool cookies slightly and roll while still warm in confectioners' sugar. Serve with a scoop of Peach Sorbet.

PEACH SORBET
Makes 1 pint

To make the simple syrup for this recipe, bring 2 cups sugar and 1½ cups water to a boil, and cook until sugar is dissolved. Let cool.

1½ cups simple syrup

2 pounds ripe peaches, peeled, pits removed, and cut into quarters

1 tablespoon freshly squeezed lemon juice

1 cinnamon stick

⅛ teaspoon powdered ginger

Pinch freshly grated nutmeg

Pinch coarse salt

2 teaspoons egg white

In a large saucepan bring simple syrup to a boil and add peaches, lemon juice, cinnamon stick, ginger, nutmeg, and salt. Cook 10 to 12 minutes over medium heat, until peaches are soft. Let the mixture cool completely; remove cinnamon stick and puree in a blender or food processor. Strain peach mixture through a sieve. Freeze in an ice cream maker according to manufacturer's instructions. Add egg white to peach mixture halfway through the freezing process.

pecan pain perdu

Makes 4 servings

Pain perdu in French translates as "lost bread," and this recipe is a clever way to use leftovers. The pecan crust on this version of French toast makes a memorable brunch dish. It is great served with warm maple syrup.

2 cups pecans, finely chopped

4 large eggs

1½ cups milk

½ cup light-brown sugar

1 teaspoon pure vanilla extract

¼ teaspoon ground cinnamon

1 tablespoon orange zest

1 loaf French bread, cut into 1-inch-thick slices

3 tablespoons unsalted butter

Preheat the oven to 350°F. Place pecans in a shallow pan or plate, and set aside. In a large bowl, whisk together eggs, and then whisk in milk, brown sugar, vanilla, cinnamon, and zest. Soak bread slices in egg mixture until soaked through, about 1 minute. Lay soaked slices on pecans, pressing nuts into bread and turn over so the pecans adhere to the other side.

Heat a large skillet over medium-high heat, and add 1½ tablespoons butter. When butter is bubbly, add as many slices as will fit in skillet with room for turning. Cook bread 2 minutes on each side, and then transfer to a baking sheet. Continue this process until all the bread slices are toasted. Transfer to the oven and bake 7 minutes, or until the bread is crisp.

confetti cornbread

Makes 8 servings

Nothing compares with warm cornbread fresh from the oven, and I couldn't write a soul food cookbook without a cornbread recipe. I can't remember many dinners growing up without it since my mother baked fresh cornbread at least three times a week. On the other days we ate the leftovers. This recipe is simple to make, with or without the colorful and tasty vegetables.

1 large egg
1½ cups buttermilk
1 cup all-purpose flour
1 cup stone-ground cornmeal
4 teaspoons baking powder
½ teaspoon baking soda
2 teaspoons coarse salt
1 tablespoon sugar
½ cup (1 stick) unsalted butter
1½ tablespoons chopped hot green chiles
1 red bell pepper, cored, seeded, and diced
3 green onions, chopped
¾ cup cooked corn kernels
Vegetable spray

In a small skillet over medium heat, melt butter and add chiles, bell pepper, and green onions. Cook 10 minutes, or until vegetables are soft. Fold the corn and pepper mixture into the batter. Remove heated skillet from oven and spray with vegetable spray. Add batter and bake 20 to 25 minutes for skillet or 10 to 15 minutes for sticks.

Preheat the oven to 425°F. Place a cast-iron skillet or corn-stick mold in an oven to heat. In a mixing bowl, whisk together egg and buttermilk. In a separate bowl, mix together flour, cornmeal, baking powder, baking soda, salt, and sugar. Add flour mixture to buttermilk mixture, and stir with a wooden spoon until batter just combines (do not overmix).

sweet potato and sage madeleines

Makes 64 miniature madeleines or 36 large madeleines

The embellishment of baked sweet potato and fresh sage in the madeleine is the New Soul twist on an historic recipe that author Marcel Proust immortalized in *Remembrance of Things Past*. The subtly sweet treat is perfect with tea, coffee, a midday treat, or as an accompaniment to ice cream or sorbet.

1 orange-fleshed sweet potato
2 large eggs
⅓ cup sugar
½ cup all-purpose flour, plus more for pan
½ teaspoon baking powder
4 tablespoons unsalted butter,
   plus more for pan
1½ tablespoons chopped sage
¼ teaspoon ground cinnamon
¼ teaspoon ground allspice
Pinch nutmeg
Pinch coarse salt

Preheat the oven to 350°F. Prick skin of sweet potato, cover in foil, and bake 1 hour. Remove from oven and let cool. Scoop out flesh of potato, puree in a food processor, and set aside.

Meanwhile, in a large bowl, whisk eggs and sugar, and slowly add flour and baking powder. Melt butter in a small saucepan and add sage, spices, salt, and sweet potato puree. Fold in the egg-flour mixture. Mix well, and then set aside to cool.

Increase oven temperature to 450°F. Grease and flour a madeleine mold. Fill mold shells to top with batter, wiping clean in between each unbaked madeleine with a paper towel. Bake 5 minutes; lower temperature to 400°F and bake an additional 5 to 7 minutes, until cakes are firm. Continue cooking until batter is finished, regreasing and flouring the molds each time.

buckwheat and chive griddle cakes

Makes 4 servings

Buckwheat flour adds density and a nutty flavor to this uncomplicated pancake recipe. These are great when served in a stack with a side of bacon or cut into bite-sized cakes for a wonderful appetizer topped with caviar.

1½ cups sifted unbleached flour
½ cup buckwheat flour
½ teaspoon coarse salt
½ teaspoon baking soda
2 teaspoons baking powder
1 large egg
2 cups buttermilk
1 tablespoon unsalted butter, melted
¼ cup chopped chives
Vegetable spray

In a medium bowl, stir together dry ingredients, and set aside. In a large bowl, beat egg and whisk in buttermilk. Slowly whisk flour mixture into buttermilk mixture and then add melted butter. Fold in chives.

Heat a griddle or heavy skillet and generously coat with vegetable spray. Add ⅓ cup griddle-cake mixture, and cook on one side until small bubbles form, about 5 minutes. Turn and cook 3 minutes on other side. Cook as many griddle cakes at a time as your griddle or skillet will hold, but do not overcrowd, so you will have room to turn them.

buttermilk biscuits

Makes 18 biscuits

The buttermilk available today is cultivated, but originally it was the liquid that remained after the milk had been churned to make butter. It adds flavor to this recipe and aids in the rising process as it reacts with the baking soda to make these biscuits extra flaky. The Curried Pear Butter on page 139 is the perfect accompaniment.

3½ cups sifted unbleached flour
2 teaspoons coarse salt
4 teaspoons baking powder
2 teaspoons sugar
1 teaspoon baking soda
1¼ cups (2½ sticks) unsalted butter
1½ cups buttermilk
Heavy cream, for brushing

Preheat the oven to 425°F. In a large bowl, whisk together dry ingredients. Using a pastry cutter, gently cut in butter until the mixture resembles small peas. Add buttermilk and mix with a wooden spoon without overworking the dough. The dough should be slightly sticky. Pour onto lightly floured counter and lightly gather until mixture just comes together. Roll to a 1-inch thickness.

Using a cookie cutter or paring knife, cut out 18 two-inch rounds and place on a nonstick cookie sheet. Refrigerate 30 minutes. Brush tops with heavy cream and bake 14 to 16 minutes, until golden brown.

homemade yeast rolls

Makes 24 rolls

I'm reminded of Miss Laura Harris, my grandmother's thoughtful neighbor, when I think of these tasty rolls. She never failed to send over a batch when my family visited from up North. Homemade breads are a lovely way to punctuate a New Soul meal. These easy rolls will complement almost any main dish in the second chapter.

1 package (¼ ounce) dry active yeast
1 cup warm water–110°F
½ cup sugar
1 large egg, beaten
2 teaspoons salt
1 cup milk, scalded
¾ cup (1½ sticks) unsalted butter, melted
5 cups flour

Preheat the oven to 425°F. In the bowl of an electric mixer fitted with the dough hook, dissolve yeast in warm water. Stir in sugar and add egg, salt, milk, and ½ cup (1 stick) melted butter. With a mixer on low speed, slowly add flour until the dough pulls together. Transfer to a floured surface, and knead dough 5 minutes. Place the dough in a large buttered bowl, cover with a kitchen towel and set in a warm place to rise until double in bulk, about 1 hour.

Lightly oil a 3-inch muffin tin. Punch down dough and form dough into 1-inch balls. Place 3 balls in each muffin tin. Cover with a kitchen towel and allow to rise ½ hour. Brush generously with the remaining melted butter. Bake in preheated oven 15 to 20 minutes, until golden brown.

pecan shortbread

Makes 32 cookies

This simple recipe is given true Southern charm with the addition of pecans. It is an example of when butter versus moderation really matters—the richness is another thing that makes the cookies so special. I like making square and triangle shaped cookies by using a sharp pairing knife. You can also use a cookie cutter.

½ **pound unsalted butter, softened**
½ **cup powdered sugar**
2 cups flour
¼ **teaspoon salt**
1 cup pecan pieces

Preheat the oven to 350°F. In the bowl of an electric mixer, cream butter and sugar. Slowly add flour, then salt. Fold in pecan pieces. Roll dough into a ball, wrap in plastic, and refrigerate 30 minutes. On a floured surface, roll dough out ¼-inch thick. Cut into desired shapes. Transfer cookies to an ungreased cookie sheet. Prick the cookies with a fork, and chill again 20 minutes. Bake 20 minutes, or until edges are lightly browned.

CONDIMENTS, relishes, DRESSINGS, vinaigrettes, SAUCES, rubs

These simple condiments for the New Soul kitchen add exponential flavors and new taste sensations. The traditional and New Soul kitchen is always filled with condiments to enhance and complement favorite dishes for a way of doctorin' it up. Most of these are extremely versatile and can be served with a variety of the recipes in the other chapters.

creole vinaigrette

Makes 1 cup

The inspiration for this vinaigrette is the strong-but-balanced flavors of Creole cooking. Many of the dishes have a combination of tomatoes, spices, and herbs. Enjoy this vinaigrette with your favorite mix of salad greens.

¼ cup tomato juice
1 tablespoon plus 1 teaspoon cider vinegar
2 tablespoon chopped shallots
1 teaspoon Dijon-style mustard
1 teaspoon Worcestershire sauce
1 teaspoon Tabasco sauce
1 teaspoon coarse salt
½ teaspoon sugar
¼ teaspoon freshly ground black pepper
¼ teaspoon paprika
⅛ teaspoon celery seed
⅛ teaspoon garlic salt
1 teaspoon chopped oregano
1 teaspoon chopped thyme
½ cup extra-virgin olive oil

In a small bowl, whisk together all ingredients except oil. Slowly whisk in oil until well combined. Store, refrigerated, in an airtight container, up to one week.

green buttermilk dressing

Makes 2 cups

Fresh herbs and buttermilk are a refreshing combination. I serve this dressing on romaine or iceberg lettuce and add croutons to soak up the dressing. Any soft herb such as tarragon, chervil, or dill can be substituted for a flavor variation.

1½ cups buttermilk
1 cup packed spinach leaves
½ cup green onions
¼ cup chopped basil
2 tablespoons chopped chives
1 teaspoon minced jalapeño chile
1 tablespoon honey
Juice of ½ lemon
Coarse salt
Freshly ground white pepper

Put buttermilk, spinach, green onions, basil, chives, jalapeño, honey, and lemon juice into a blender, and puree. Season with salt and white pepper to taste. Store, refrigerated, in an airtight container, up to one week.

dry jamaican jerk spices

Makes ⅔ cup

Spice blends are common on supermarket shelves these days, but you can easily make your own. Adding Jamaican jerk spices to your repertoire will make you extremely popular around the grill.

2 teaspoons cayenne pepper
4 teaspoons ground allspice
2 teaspoons ground nutmeg
1 teaspoon ground cascabel chile
  (or other hot chile)
2 teaspoons ground cinnamon
1 tablespoon garlic powder
1 tablespoon onion powder
2 tablespoons coarse salt
1 teaspoon fresly ground black pepper

Place all ingredients into a small bowl, and stir to combine. Store in an airtight container for up to three months.

new soul hot red-pepper sauce

Makes 1½ cups

Every household should have its own hot-sauce recipe. If you look at the shelves in specialty food markets nowadays, you'd think this was already the case. One reason for the huge number of hot sauces is the many varieties of chiles; each has its unique level of heat and flavor.

1 red onion, minced
1⅓ cups champagne vinegar
1 tablespoon brown sugar
3 red bell peppers, roasted, cored,
  and seeded
1 heaping tablespoon roasted garlic
  (see instructions, page 98)
1 tablespoon chipotle chile puree
¼ teaspoon cayenne pepper
⅛ teaspoon ground allspice
1 teaspoon coarse salt

Place onion, ⅔ cup vinegar, and brown sugar in a small pot, and bring to a boil. Reduce to medium heat, and cook 10 minutes. Add peppers, garlic, chile puree, spices, and salt; continue to cook, stirring constantly for 5 minutes. Let cool and puree in a blender. Store, refrigerated, in an airtight container, up to two weeks.

curried pear butter

Makes 1 pint

Cooked fruit butters in the New Soul kitchen are similar to compotes and are typically served with biscuits and breads. The addition of curry powder gives this pear butter a West Indian spin.

3 pounds pears (preferably Anjou)
1½ cups water
1 cup cider vinegar
¾ cup sugar
2 tablespoons freshly squeezed lemon juice
1 heaping teaspoon curry powder
¼ teaspoon ground cinnamon
½ teaspoon coarse salt

Chop unpeeled pears into a medium dice, and add to a large pot. Cover the pears with the water and vinegar, and cook until they are very soft, about 30 minutes. Strain and press pears through a fine sieve or food mill, and return pear puree to pot. Add sugar, lemon juice, spices, and salt, and cook mixture for about 1 hour or until the consistency of ketchup. Store, refrigerated, in an airtight container, up to two weeks.

spicy rémoulade

Makes 1½ cups

The origin of this mayonnaise-based sauce is French, a cuisine that greatly influences my New Soul kitchen. I like the taste of salty capers and anchovies, especially when served with fresh seafood.

1 cup homemade or prepared mayonnaise
1 teaspoon Dijon-style mustard
1½ tablespoons capers
2 tablespoons chopped parsley
2 tablespoons chopped tarragon
2 teaspoons paprika
1 teaspoon cayenne pepper
Juice of 1 lemon
1 clove garlic
2 anchovy fillets or 1 teaspoon anchovy paste
Dash Worcestershire sauce
Coarse salt
Freshly ground white pepper

Mix mayonnaise, mustard, capers, parsley, tarragon, paprika, cayenne, lemon juice, garlic, anchovies, and Worcestershire sauce in food processor. Season with salt and white pepper to taste. Store, refrigerated, in an airtight container, up to one week.

roasted tomato mayonnaise

Makes 2 cups

My parents tell me they were raised eating tomato and mayonnaise sandwiches. Although I believe this was told to me for dramatic effect, the two ingredients are nonetheless a pleasant combination.

8 plum tomatoes
1 tablespoon light-brown sugar
Coarse salt
Freshly ground white pepper
3 cloves garlic
2 tablespoons fresh thyme
Extra-virgin olive oil, for drizzling
1½ cups prepared mayonnaise
3 tablespoons ketchup
1 tablespoon Dijon-style mustard
1 teaspoon paprika

Preheat the oven to 250°F. Cut plum tomatoes in half, and place on a cookie sheet with cut side up. Sprinkle tomatoes with brown sugar, and salt and pepper to taste. Slice garlic and scatter on top of tomatoes. Sprinkle tomatoes with thyme, and drizzle with olive oil. Bake tomatoes 6 hours, until most of the moisture has evaporated and skins are wrinkled. Allow to cool.

In a blender, combine mayonnaise, tomatoes, ketchup, mustard, and paprika. Season with salt and white pepper to taste. Store, refrigerated, in an airtight container, up to one week.

piccalilli julienne

Makes 6 servings

This condiment is quite typical in the soul food pantry—a pickle or relish is never too far away from a pot of greens or fresh steamed or grilled fish. You'll often find the combination of salty, sour, and sweet with a little spice not too far behind.

1 green bell pepper, cored, seeded, and julienned
2 medium zucchini, sliced into half moons
1 yellow onion, cut in half and thinly sliced
1 jalapeño chile, julienned
½ cup coarse salt
½ cup cider vinegar
1 cup light-brown sugar
1 teaspoon celery seeds
1 teaspoon mustard seeds
1 teaspoon ground ginger
1 cinnamon stick
½ teaspoon ground turmeric
2 bay leaves
¼ teaspoon whole cloves
½ teaspoon whole black peppercorns

Place bell pepper, zucchini, onion, jalapeño, and ½ cup salt in a medium bowl. Transfer to the refrigerator and let chill overnight. Drain and rinse vegetables, and place in heatproof bowl. Place vinegar, brown sugar, celery and mustard seeds, ginger, cinnamon stick, turmeric, bay leaves, cloves, and black peppercorns in a medium saucepan, and bring to a boil. Pour over vegetables, and allow to cool. Store, refrigerated, in an airtight container, up to two weeks.

tropical salsa

Makes 6½-cup servings

This refreshing salsa is a great cooling side dish for several of the spicy dishes, such as Piri Piri Grilled Shrimp on page 37, or Island-Spiced Braised Beef Short Ribs on page 38. Use the ripest and juiciest fruit that you can find for the best results. Carambola, also known as star fruit, has a crunchy texture when ripe and a flavor somewhere between an apple and a melon.

2 carambolas, cut into ¼-inch dice
1 mango, cut into ¼-inch dice
1 guava, cut into ¼-inch dice
½ papaya, cut into ¼-inch dice
1 jalapeño chile, seeded and minced
¼ cup minced red onion
¼ cup chopped cilantro leaves, plus more
  for garnish
3 tablespoons freshly squeezed lime juice
2 tablespoons extra-virgin olive oil
Coarse salt
Freshly ground white pepper

Mix carambolas, mango, guava, papaya, jalapeño, onion, cilantro leaves, lime juice, and olive oil in a large bowl, and season with salt and white pepper to taste. Garnish with cilantro leaves, if desired. Use immediately.

roasted corn relish

Makes 6½-cup servings

It's very easy to play "relish roulette." Just remember to use about 2 cups of a main ingredient (such as roasted, cubed beets or chopped peppers), ½ cup or so of your onion of choice (green onions, red onions, shallots), acid (vinegar of choice or citrus juice), some heat (jalapeño or serrano chiles), fresh herbs, a little oil, and salt and pepper. This recipe is extra special when using seasonally fresh corn. If you wish, you can boil or grill the corn instead of roasting it.

4 ears corn, in husks
1 red onion, minced
1 cup packed chopped parsley leaves
1 tablespoon chopped jalapeño
2 tablespoons red-wine vinegar
¼ cup extra-virgin olive oil
½ teaspoon honey
Coarse salt
Freshly ground white pepper

Preheat the oven to 350°F. Fill the bottom of a baking sheet with ¼ inch water, and place corn on bottom. Cook 20 minutes, or until kernels are just tender (you will need to pull back the husk to test); do not overcook. The water should be mostly evaporated. Cut kernels from the cob, and transfer to a large bowl. Add onion, parsley, jalapeño, vinegar, olive oil, and honey, and mix well. Season with salt and white pepper to taste. Use immediately.

jícama-papaya slaw

Makes 6 servings

The jícama is an unfamiliar root vegetable to many people in the United States. It has a thin, beige skin; a potato-like flesh; and an apple-like taste. Once you experience its delightful versatility, you're likely to begin using it in salads. Try to find a ripe and juicy papaya to contrast with the crunchy texture of the jícama.

½ medium-sized jícama
1 papaya
1 orange, cut into segments
3 green onions, sliced thin
1 bunch cilantro, stems removed
½ pound spinach, stems removed
1 tablespoon seeded, chopped jalapeño chiles
½ cup fresly squeezed orange juice
1 tablespoon freshly squeezed lime juice
⅔ cup canola or vegetable oil
Honey
Coarse salt
Freshly ground white pepper

Using a vegetable peeler, peel jícama and slice into thin pieces; cut into thin strips. Using a paring knife, peel papaya, cut in half and remove seeds. Slice papaya in thin strips, and then toss together in a large bowl with the jícama. Toss orange segments and green onions into jícama mixture.

In a blender, add cilantro and spinach leaves, jalapeño, and orange and lime juices. Slowly drizzle in oil, and season with honey, salt, and white pepper to taste. Dress the jícama-papaya mixture with cilantro-spinach mixture, and serve immediately.

green chile harissa sauce

Makes 4 servings

This North African–inspired condiment is usually made with red peppers and red chiles and often accompanies couscous. The heat of the poblano chile varies, so give the sauce a taste test before you pour it on.

2 poblano chiles

1 jalapeño chile

⅓ cup plus 3 tablespoons olive oil

½ teaspoon coarse salt, plus more
    for sprinkling

⅛ teaspoon freshly ground black pepper,
    plus more for sprinkling

1 onion, finely chopped

1 tablespoon chopped garlic

1 teaspoon chopped fresh thyme

⅛ teaspoon ground turmeric

⅛ teaspoon ground cinnamon

Pinch ground cloves

2 tablespoons chopped mint

1 teaspoon honey

Preheat the oven to 400°F. Wash and then dry poblano and jalapeño chiles, and toss with 1 tablespoon olive oil and a sprinkling of salt and pepper. Wrap in foil and roast 1 hour. When the chiles have cooled, remove their thin skin, seeds, and stem.

Meanwhile, heat a small skillet and add 2 tablespoons olive oil. Cook onions and garlic until soft and translucent, 5 to 7 minutes. Stir in thyme, turmeric, cinnamon, cloves, and mint, and allow mixture to cool. In a food processor, blend onion mixture, chiles, and honey. Drizzle in remaining ⅓ cup oil, and season with salt and black pepper to taste. Store, refrigerated, in an airtight container, up to three days.

pecan, herb, and spinach pesto

Makes 1½ cups

This pesto is more economical than traditional pesto, since it's made mostly with spinach and pecans. The hearty pecans also add more texture than the smooth pine nuts. This is a great sauce for pasta or a dipping sauce for vegetables.

¾ cup pecans, toasted
1 cup packed basil leaves
¼ cup parsley leaves
2 cups packed spinach leaves, washed, stemmed, and torn into small pieces
½ cup Parmesan cheese
¼ cup freshly squeezed lemon juice
1 tablespoon minced garlic
½ cup extra-virgin olive oil
½ teaspoon coarse salt
¼ teaspoon freshly ground pepper

Place ingredients in a food processor, and blend. Store, refrigerated, in an airtight container, up to three days.

west african peanut sauce

Makes 1 quart

Peanuts were introduced to the Africans and Europeans during the transatlantic slave trade from the 1520s to the 1860s and soon became a popular commodity. As with most nuts, they adapt to both sweet and savory recipes. This flavorful sauce is also great tossed with rice noodles or vermicelli.

1 teaspoon coarse salt, plus more to taste
4 plum tomatoes
1½ cups natural peanut butter
1 cup coconut milk
½ cup water
2 tablespoons chopped ginger
1 tablespoon chopped garlic
1 tablespoon fish sauce
1 tablespoon chopped jalapeño chile
Juice of 1 lime
½ teaspoon ground cumin
3 green onions, finely chopped
1 cup chopped cilantro leaves
Freshly ground white pepper

Prepare an ice bath. Bring a small pot of water to boil and add 1 teaspoon salt. Remove stem end from tomatoes, and with a paring knife, slice an X on the other end. Add tomatoes to boiling water; remove them as soon as the skin begins to peel away, about 1 minute. Drain, and immediately plunge tomatoes in ice water. Drain again, and remove skin of tomatoes. Cut tomatoes into quarters, scoop out seeds, and dice.

In a large bowl, whisk together peanut butter, coconut milk, and the water. Stir in ginger, garlic, fish sauce, jalapeño, lime juice, cumin, green onions, and cilantro. Season with salt and white pepper to taste.

suggested reading

There have been many chefs and cookbook authors who have inspired me over the years. I've listed a few of my favorite publications that I've turned to many times during the development of this book.

Kwame Anthony Appiah and Henry Louis Gates, Jr. *Africana, The Encyclopedia of the African and African-American Experience*. New York: Basic Civitas Books, 1999.

Sarah Belk. *Around the Southern Table*. New York: Simon & Schuster, 1991.

Alan Davidson. *The Oxford Companion to Food*. New York: Oxford University Press, 1999.

Damon Lee Fowler. *Classical Southern Cooking*. New York: Crown Publishers, Inc., 1995.

Camille Glenn. *The Heritage of Southern Cooking*. New York: Workman Publishing, Inc., 1986.

Sharon Tyler Herbst. *Food Lover's Companion*, Hauppauge, New York: Barron's Educational Series, Inc., 2001.

Emeril Lagasse and Jessie Tirch. *Emeril's New New Orleans Cooking*. New York: William Morrow and Company, Inc., 1993

Paula Lalbachan. *The Complete Caribbean Cookbook*. Rutland, Vermont: Charles E. Tuttle Co., Inc., 1994.

Larousse Gastronomique, edited by Jennifer Lang. New York: Crown Publishers, Inc., 1984.

Edna Lewis. *The Taste of Country Cooking*. New York: Alfred A. Knopf, 1996.

Jill Norman. *The Complete Book of Spices*, New York: Viking Studio Books, 1990.

James Peterson. *Fish & Shellfish*. New York: William Morrow and Company, Inc., 1996.

Chris Schlesinger and John Willoughby, *How to Cook Meat*. New York: William Morrow and Company, Inc., 2000.

Elizabeth Schneider. *Uncommon Fruits & Vegetables*. New York: Harper & Row, Publishers, 1986.

John Martin Taylor. *Hoppin' John's Low Country Cooking*. New York: Bantam Books, 1992.

Elizabeth Terry. *Savannah Seasons*. New York: Doubleday, 1996.

The Visual Food Encyclopedia, New York: MacMillan, 1996.

Anne Willan. *La Varenne Pratique*. New York: Crown Publishers, Inc., 1989.

Paula Wolfert. *Paula Wolfert's World of Food*. New York: Harper & Row, Publishers, 1988.

metric conversion charts

WEIGHT EQUIVALENTS

The metric weights given in this chart are not exact equivalents, but have been rounded up or down slightly to make measuring easier.

Avoirdupois	Metric
¼ oz	7 g
½ oz	15 g
1 oz	30 g
2 oz	60 g
3 oz	90 g
4 oz	115 g
5 oz	150 g
6 oz	175 g
7 oz	200 g
8 oz (½ lb)	225 g
9 oz	250 g
10 oz	300 g
11 oz	325 g
12 oz	350 g
13 oz	375 g
14 oz	400 g
15 oz	425 g
16 oz (1 lb)	450 g
1½ lb	675 g
2 lb	900 g
2¼ lb	1 kg
3 lb	1.4 kg
4 lb	1.8 kg

VOLUME EQUIVALENTS

These are not exact equivalents for American cups and spoons, but have been rounded up or down slightly to make measuring easier.

American	Metric	Imperial
¼ t	1.2 ml	
½ t	2.5 ml	
1 t	5.0 ml	
½ T (1.5 t)	7.5 ml	
1 T (3 t)	15 ml	
¼ cup (4 T)	60 ml	2 fl oz
⅓ cup (5 T)	75 ml	2½ fl oz
½ cup (8 T)	125 ml	4 fl oz
⅔ cup (10 T)	150 ml	5 fl oz
¾ cup (12 T)	175 ml	6 fl oz
1 cup (16 T)	250 ml	8 fl oz
1¼ cups	300 ml	10 fl oz (½ pt)
1½ cups	350 ml	12 fl oz
2 cups (1 pint)	500 ml	16 fl oz
2½ cups	625 ml	20 fl oz (1 pint)
1 quart	1 liter	32 fl oz

OVEN TEMPERATURE EQUIVALENTS

Oven Mark	F	C	Gas
Very cool	250–275	130–140	½–1
Cool	300	150	2
Warm	325	170	3
Moderate	350	180	4
Moderately hot	375	190	5
	400	200	6
Hot	425	220	7
	450	230	8
Very hot	475	250	9

index

index

acknowledgments

Hollis and Annette Holland, my parents. It all began with you, your open-minded approach to life and your curiosity about the foods of other cultures. The dinners in and out, the road trips across the country, the moving around, the trip to Russia, and supporting my desire to go to "graduate" school in France. Thank you for providing me with an amazing foundation and telling me that I could be whatever I wanted to be.

To Janelle Holland, my little sister who has always been my most important food critic. I love you very much. To my many aunts and uncles and who have encouraged and inspired me through all my incarnations: Maxine and Don Jones, Elaine and Matt Halley, Mary and Cornell Wilson, Essie and Al Coleman, Arlean and Bob Wilson, Martha and Dawud Mateen, Larry Thomas, Don Thomas, and Dan Holland. To special cousins: Charles Fisher; Reva and George Robinson; Daphne Jones; Najeeba and Fatima Mateen; Cory, Caren, and Candace Wilson. And to family friends: Judy and Moses Gilbert, Charles and Marge Champion, Phil Sitton, Natalie and Reverend Dwight Cook.

This book is also for my soulful friends. To those who have been there through the good, as well as the bad, times: Andy and Karen Sarnow and Annie Powell. Thank you for your unconditional love and support.

Where would I be without the laughter and love provided by Robert Britt, Ellen Mayock and Pat Bradley, Robert and Lesley Driver Lawson, Michael Green, Marisa Scali, Jeanne Hardy, Darcy Elliot, Dorcey Berndt, Anna Bottoroff, José Oliver, John and Beth Caban, Thor Christenson, Brian Brown, Shelley Pyne-Hanley, JoAnna Noble and Gordon Runté, Hannah Dexter, Erik and Rhonda Albert, Sean and Julia Farley, Jason Holmes, Alison Justus, Erin and John Larkin, Andy Fekula, Andrea Boccacino, Cynthia Tindale and Patrick Ferencz, and all my recipe testers and tasters. And, Josephine Pagani and Paula Cerrone, thanks for those first cookbooks and dinner parties.

To my godson Jake Henning: I will always be inspired to be a better person because of you. Thank you Staci and Joe for this gift.

Special thanks to Denise and Christine Corcoran and Greg Scott for providing me with extraordinary hospitality whenever I'm in New York.

Recipe testers and tasters: Rebecca Friend, Kelsey Lane, Elizabeth Olsen, Peggy Liu and Rob McCormick, Marianna Marino, John Baccio, Charles Darwall and Tora Stoneman, Abby O'Leary and Jack Bailey, Staci, Joseph, Jake, and Samara Henning, Gail Siddle and family, Lisa and Marc Herrenbruck, Lisa Harrington, Barb Walkowski, Andy Lax, Art Herrera, Jeff and Tamar Culberson, and Jeffrey Leiken. And special thanks to Tuffy Eldridge for being a devoted fan.

Food writing colleagues: Don Fry, Deborah Grossman, Tori Ritchie, Diane Morgan, Toni Allegra, Jeannette Ferrary, and Sally Schneider. Thank you for encouraging me to pursue this project and find my voice in this field. And to the 2002 Greenbrier Symposium participants.

Brian Maynard at KitchenAid, thanks for the kitchen tools. Alicia Engstrom at Tsar Nicolai Caviar, thanks for your delicious product and support. And, to Konstantine Mironychev at M.A.C, my multi-talented makeup artist friend.

Lastly, but certainly not least, to the team that made this book happen: Lisa Ekus, book agent extraordinaire. Thank you for your professionalism, super-quick response time, unparalleled wisdom, and advice for not only this book but also other aspects of my career, and for your friendship. Thanks for seeing my vision and letting me run with it.

To Stewart, Tabori & Chang's publisher, Leslie Stoker, and senior editor Sandy Gilbert (the editor of this project). Many thanks to you both for also seeing my vision and giving me the tools to realize this project, which was once just a dream. I am grateful for your generosity and for this wonderful opportunity. The support staff that you provided me with has enhanced the project more than I could expect. Webster Williams is the copy editor that I want to go with me wherever I go. Thank you for your ease to work with and for protecting my voice. Nina Barnett, the book designer, thank you for interpreting my flavor palette into a visually exciting book. This book became complete with Ellen Silverman's stunning photographs and Susie Theodorou's and John Bjostad's impeccable food styling. Thank you all for your excellent work and interest.

I hope that I haven't forgotten anyone. I have crossed a lot of paths in this profession and I am grateful for every experience.